A pooch's guide to dogs behaving badly

A pooch's guide to dogs behaving badly

Robyn Osborne

www.bigskypublishing.com.au

Big Sky Publishing Pty Ltd
PO Box 303
Newport, NSW, 2106
Australia

Phone: (61 2) 9918 2168
Fax: (61 2) 9918 2396
Email: info@bigskypublishing.com.au
Web: www.bigskypublishing.com.au

The National Library of Australia Cataloguing-in-Publication entry
Osborne, Robyn.
Dog logic : a pooch's guide to dogs behaving badly
ISBN: 9780980814026
Dogs--Training.
Dogs--Behavior.
Human-animal relationships.
Dewey Number: 636.7083

Senior Editor Sharon Evans
Edit by Denise Imwold
Proofreading: Denise Imwold
Cover and layout design by Think Productions
Typesetting by Think Productions
Printed in Australia by Ligare Pty Ltd

To Dave and John, for their support and encouragement.
Also to Sox, Snowy and all the other furry
four legged 'friends' that have enriched my life.

CONTENTS

THE FIRST BARK

Hello and welcome to *Dog Logic:* the creative genius of Sox the 'Philosophical Pooch' and me, his hardworking human assistant, Robyn. Our writing partnership came about through a shared belief that every dog, regardless of background, has a book inside them. Having had some publishing success as the Philosophical Pooch in *bark! Australia* magazine, Sox was keen to once again share his wit and wisdom with the dog-loving public. *Dog Logic* is the result. As a mature mutt of 12, Sox has gained valuable life experiences and can relate closely to the common dog. This book is not academic theory dispensed from an ivory kennel, but practical, home-dug advice on raising happy and healthy dogs. It covers a diverse range of topics from barking, beds and biting, to worrisome walks and everything in between.

There was also a very practical reason for our collaboration. Although keyboards and paws do not mix, Sox refused to let his lack of fingers and opposable thumbs stop him from achieving his goal. Enter me, the helpful human, to translate and type up Sox's ruminations into the little gem you are now reading. As dog-authored books are as scarce as perspicacious pussy cats, Sox thought the readers may be interested in the daily process which resulted in *Dog Logic*, and his thoughts for future projects:

Rise, yard ablutions, perimeter check, greet humans, sun snooze, drink of water, perimeter check, sun snooze, morning tea wee, perimeter check, sun snooze ...and so on throughout the day. While sun snoozing may sound relaxing, this was the time I 'channeled' my thoughts and ideas for Dog Logic to my human. My body may have been in repose, but my mind was a buzz of activity!

I am a busy dog with a full schedule of commitments, but feel I have the perfect work/life balance. My kennel mate Snowy and I job-share the guarding duties, which allows me time for more intellectual pursuits. And as for retirement... dig a hole and bury that thought! I have so much more to achieve in life before I would even consider putting my paws up.

Sox may be a clever and eloquent canine, but at our place this doesn't make him unique. Snowy also has literary aspirations. She has made valuable contributions to *Dog Logic*, as well as penning *Midget Bones' Diary–Memoirs of a Mongrel*, her racy, risqué (and yet to be published) autobiography. As with many high-achieving individuals, there is an element of professional jealousy between them. Luckily, I, at least, have no problems being overshadowed and am happy to bask in the brilliance of my two talented and delightful canine companions.

Snowy and Sox are both ex RSPCA puppies of indeterminate heritage. We adopted Snowy in 1995 and three years later, Sox joined our family. Apart from sharing a difficult start to life, a love of chicken and intense dislike for the neighbour's cat, they are the yin and yang of the canine world, natural dualities and opposite in many ways. This is aptly revealed by examining their professional résumés:

Name	Sox
Gender	male
Age	12
Breed	Cattle Dog, Kelpie, Boxer, Doberman with a touch of water buffalo
Coat	short and glossy black
Size	large and cuddly
Tail	stumpy, yet expressive
Gait	lumbering
Characteristics	laid back, easy going
Academic record	obedience school graduate
Employment	guard dog, specialising in burglar detection
Publication history	'Philosophical Pooch' column in bi-monthly dog magazine, Dog Logic book
Hobbies	food, tummy rubs, dozing, reflective bone chews
Peer assessment	the dog most likely
Mantra	'to err is feline, to forgive canine'

Name	Snowy or Snow
Gender	female
Age	15
Breed	Terrier cross
Coat	short and snowy white
Size	petite
Tail	long and whippy
Gait	jaunty
Characteristics	frenetic, energetic and athletic
Academic record	home schooled
Employment	guard dog, specialising in rat and cat removal
Publication history	nil but ever hopeful
Hobbies	chasing bees, birds, cats and anything that moves
Peer assessment	a dog of very little brain
Mantra	'behind every great dog is an even greater bitch'

So, is Sox, the author of a book on dogs behaving badly, the perfect pooch? Can he live in a glass kennel and cast the first stone? As the human who knows him best, the answer is definitely no. Sox has his foibles, flaws and favourites as much as the next canine. His liking for chicken goes beyond mere survival. Poodles, Samoyeds, Rottweilers and baths are top of his 'to avoid' list. He has never forgotten his humble beginnings and barracks unashamedly for the underdog.

This, of course, is the point of *Dog Logic*. It is Sox's view of the world: irreverent, honest, fun, naughty, at times a little rude, but always with tongue firmly planted in muzzle. And to prove Sox is a dog with a heart as big as his tummy, he has invited the delightful canine-centred Sylvia from Bark Busters to share the *Dog Logic* stage. Sylvia and Sox have the same passion, commitment and drive to improve humans' understanding of the dog world. Being the experts in the field of dog behaviour, Bark Busters finish each chapter with the human perspective: balanced, fair and the ideal foil to Sox's unique and idiosyncratic outlook.

Sox and I had a great time creating *Dog Logic* together. In amongst all the pats, ear caresses and tummy rubs, progress was made and eventually the book emerged. It isn't the great Australian (Cattle Dog) novel. Nor does it claim to be a complete dissertation on the canine world. We hope you find *Dog Logic* entertaining, engaging and enlightening and that in some way, our little book helps you learn more about your canine companion.

Robyn Osborne

1 One Dog, Two Dog, Old Dog, New Dog

🐾 Sox's paws for thought

Dogs – more dogs the merrier
Humans – one dog is quite enough

If you have picked up this book, chances are you have a dog or are thinking about getting one. If you are already gladdened by the addition of at least one dog in your household, my question is this: how much happier would you be with a second dog? And to those poor, sad dogless readers, I'm sure you have come to realise just how empty your lives are. Yes, you do need a canine chum to feel complete (remember that children are simply noisy dog substitutes).

We dogs offer loyalty, companionship and unconditional love. There is also ample evidence to prove just how good canines are for people's health, both physiological and psychological. In short, a dog is a wet-nosed, soft-eared, wagging health elixir. Still not convinced a dog is the answer? Let me illustrate using my mathematical equation, which I have taken the liberty to name Sox's DDF (Double Dog Fun) Theorem:

If 1 x 🐕 = fun, then 2 x 🐕 🐕 = double fun

To prove I am not all smoke and mirrors, my human has put the theory to the test and can confirm it really works. Indeed, she was so impressed with my DDF, she has written about her experience in *A Tale of Two Puppies*, starring Snowy and yours truly.

One dog or two?

Remember, one dog is lonely, two's company and three's a pack. We dogs are social creatures, so a second dog is definitely worth considering. This is especially true if you are away from home a lot. Those long hours can seem interminable to a lonely pooch. Ideally, get your second dog after dog number one has settled in, as our humans did.

When I joined the Osborne household as the 'other dog', Snowy was three—mature and sensible—without being too set in her ways. She accompanied the family to the Noosa RSPCA and gave me the paws up, although in all the excitement of leaving the puppy pens, I remember little of that first meeting. I was young, confused and impressionable when I arrived at my new home, and Snowy made the most of this, as her diary excerpts reveal:

> I ran through my fair, but firm kennel rules with the youngster: no whining, no whimpering, no puddles, no belching or passing wind (unless by prior arrangement), no parties, no visits by the opposite sex after 5 pm, no felines between the hours of 100 hours and 2400 hours, and, under no circumstances, is Teddy Toy to be touched, licked or chewed. The pup has been named Sox, a highly appropriate name, as his head is full of wool. He is under the misapprehension it's because of his 'cute little sock-like paws.' Oh, pleeease....

For the record (and confirmed by my human) it really was because of my 'cute little sock-like paws' and I have never been remotely interested in having anything to do with her nasty Teddy Toy.

Before you rush off to the pound, however, please consider that not all new dogs are welcomed by the canine incumbent. Some misguided humans decide to get a puppy, just as their devoted canine is entering the twilight years. The idea being that the mature dog will happily take 'Newbie' under their paws and teach him good habits. Snowy and I have had many hypothetical 'what if' discussions on this very situation and have decided it is a load of cats' swill. While there may be some accommodating souls around, we would be most displeased, as would most dogs looking forward to a peaceful retirement, if a puppy came into our household.

'Newbie' might be a winsome ball of cuteness to you, but to the senior statesdog, he is an annoying irritant. Climbing all over a dog's human and possessions, and getting all the tasty table scraps—there's bound to be some resentment. I'm getting hot under the collar just thinking about it. If you are definite about a new puppy, please show some respect for Fido's faithful service and wait until he has moved on to a higher astral plain (one free from annoying youngsters).

Puppies

When most humans think about getting a dog, they usually think puppies, all sweet furry faces and roly-poly bodies. I call this the Power of the Puppy. Puppy Power is all about being SO cute and cuddly, that humans find them irresistible. Here are some pros and cons to think about before getting a puppy:

Puppy pros (apart from being cute and cuddly):

• no learned bad habits or emotional baggage
• lots of energy and exuberance for life

It is an interesting phenomenon that puppies have innate radars to detect which human needs to be charmed. It is one of the essential survival tactics learnt in early puppyhood. Consequently, when Snowy was chosen to join the Osborne household as a youngster, she knew exactly who to target:

The female human and young male were putty in my delicate paws. I ignored them. It was the big male who needed work. I used all my winsome puppy ways and in no time I'd won him over completely. I changed him from a 'no dog' to 'pro dog' person within a week.

Puppy cons:

- destructive behaviour (digging, chewing, scratching)
- demanding of human time
- not toilet trained
- not obedience trained
- not de-sexed

Snowy has publicly issued a guilty plea to all five counts of puppy misdemeanors, but hopes the readers understand these occurred many years ago in her carefree youth (or so she maintains).

The older dog

But what about the forgotten older canine as a suitable adoptee? These dogs often end up in pounds or shelters through no fault of their own and there are some compelling reasons why humans should consider the more mature, but still 'young at heart'. While the oldies lack the cuteness factor, they are less work.

Senior dogs are generally:

- de-sexed (hopefully)
- housetrained (hopefully)
- over the difficult puppy age, so more settled
- competent in basic obedience training
- less demanding of human time

Just as there are issues with puppies, older dogs have problems inherent with their age, as Snowy and I are discovering to our dismay with each passing year:

- possible health issues (arthritis, hearing and eyesight problems, kidney disease)
- pre-existing behaviour problem (emotional baggage)
- an unknown past

My human assistant volunteered to do some on-line research into adopting older dogs. After just a few minutes of viewing grizzled muzzles and sad eyes, she became quite emotional. There was even some crazy talk about adopting the lot of them. Luckily common sense triumphed. You can only fit so many dogs on a suburban block of land.

As to my personal recommendation, I am keeping my muzzle out of this one. The one dog or two, puppy or senior decision has to be yours alone. Ultimately, it comes down to personal choice. All I ask is that you think very carefully before committing to your new canine chum/s, be they young, old or in between. After all, they want to be your companion for life.

Many paws make light work.

The Human Perspective on Your Perfect Match

Many people ask our therapists if they should purchase one or two dogs, a pre-loved older dog or a puppy, or provide a companion for a dog they already have (as in the case of Sox and Snowy). Selecting the right dog is no easy task and should be considered carefully.

Before you proceed headlong into any decision to adopt, allowing your heart to rule your head, I advise you to first look very closely at your lifestyle, the amount of space you have, the time you can devote and what impact your eventual selection will make on your life. Dogs are pack animals and have four basic needs – food, shelter, leadership/companionship and entertainment – and they look to us as their pack leaders to fulfil these needs. To assist you with your choice, I have listed the following options:

One new puppy

A new puppy has similar needs to a new baby in the household. He needs four feeds daily, constant care, companionship and education. Remember puppies are very active; they chew and need toilet training, to mention just a few of their characteristics.

Two new puppies

As you've probably guessed, in getting two new puppies you've certainly upped the ante in juggling your work-life-dog balance. Two new babies in the household are double the fun but also double the trouble. The benefit of two puppies is that they'll have each other for companionship, which is a must when you have a busy lifestyle, but it would be unfair to leave them to their own devices for hours on end. You will still have to nurture your puppies and this takes time and effort. If you cut corners you will probably end up with problems such as barking, fighting and general disobedience when they mature.

Three or more puppies

An option not for the faint hearted. This is far too much work for the inexperienced, and not something I would recommend. You need to stop at two puppies, but can add another puppy down the track if you really want to have more than two.

Mature full-grown dog/dogs

They are usually already toilet trained, they require only one meal a day, and you can assess their size and the level of energy and care required. In essence, you already have the finished article that might need some training, but requires nowhere near as much care as puppies.

If you do decide to acquire two dogs/pups, it's best to choose one of each sex, mainly because two of the same sex can become competitive and fights could occur. There is far less chance of sibling rivalry when you have a boy and a girl, and on the rare occasions when they do fight, the male usually concedes (don't they always?). If you are adamant about getting two of the same sex, then make sure that you have both of them de-sexed. Also ensure you only select dogs or puppies of comparable size. To avoid problems occurring, it is also imperative that you treat both dogs equally and do not favour one over the other, as this can create problems such as sibling rivalry.

When Sisters Fight

I was called in to treat a chronic case of sibling rivalry in a family where two large female dogs, Bonnie and Tara, (that had lived happily together for many years) had recently begun fighting. The cause was that one of them had taken ill, and the owners had begun to favour the sick dog over the healthy dog. This resulted in an inequality in the pack, so the fighting began.

I firstly set about explaining the dynamics of pack structure. Because the humans favoured one dog (the underdog) over the other dog (the more dominant one) they had inadvertently caused instability of the pack. They had to reverse this by treating both of them equally, and the dogs would then fall naturally into line and balance would be restored.

I showed the owners how to become the alpha human in simple ways, such as by going in front of the dog when approaching doorways, when moving from one room to the other, and when going up and down stairs. This subliminally conveys to a dog that the humans are in charge. Bonnie and Tara have stopped fighting and now live happily together.

Bark Busters say:

- Analyse your lifestyle and the amount of space you have before deciding on one or more puppies or dogs.

- If selecting more than one puppy or dog, it's best to choose one of each sex, as two of the same sex may develop sibling rivalry.

- If you're adamant about adopting two of the same sex, select two of equal size.

- Always pick up your new dog or puppy early in the day as this gives them time to settle in, and disruptions to your sleep will be less likely.

- Settle your puppy/dog into his new bed from day one.

- Don't rush to your puppy/dog the instant he begins to bark or cry; instead call out a verbal correction, letting him know you are still there.

- If you decide to allow your new dog or puppy to sleep in your room, then make sure he has his own bed. Allowing him into your bed could create behavioural problems.

- Adhere to original diet initially, and make any diet change gradual.

- Always supply plenty of fresh water, warm bedding, companionship and leadership.

2 Breeding, Bitsers and Bluebloods

🐾 Sox's paws for thought

Dogs – handsome is as handsome does
Humans – handsome is as handsome looks

In this chapter, I hope to demystify and explore the big question facing humans. No, not the 'does space ever end?' or 'what is the meaning of life?' dilemmas. These are of passing interest to a philosophical pooch of my intellect, but what I really want to sink my teeth into is the real enigma in life—bitser or blueblood— which is best? Should you, the potential dog-owning human, purchase a bitser (also called mongrel, mutt or mixed breed) or blueblood (also called pedigree or purebred)? Of course, nothing in life is that simple (apart from a Poodle's brain) and there are pros and cons on both sides of the dog fence.

You can pick up a canine chum for next to nothing or spend a King Charles Cavalier's ransom. Being an ex-pound puppy of unknown heritage, I am a proud graduate from the school of hard yaps and a staunch supporter of the mongrel mob. On the other paw, I am not part of the rabid 'bitsers are best, forget the rest' movement, unlike a certain kennel mate, keen to use this chapter as a forum for her radical views. Indeed, some of my best friends are bluebloods and I feel I can mix it with the best of breeds. Unfortunately, class consciousness is alive and well in the canine fraternity and certain dogs do look down their genetically refined muzzles at the ubiquitous mongrel. (Yes, I think Shadow does know we mean him, Snow.) Like any dog, I have my dislikes (Poodles, Samoyeds and Rottweilers spring to mind) and favourites (nearly every other dog) and for this I make no apology.

Breeding

First up, is that hoary old chestnut, are mongrels hardier and healthier than purebreds? Sorry pedigree pals, but the general consensus amongst 'those in the know' is that we most definitely are. Even though purebred dogs can trace their ancestry a long way back, chances are Snowy and I will enjoy better health and live longer. This is due to our 'hybrid vigour' and 'genetic diversity'—fancy scientific terms for having relatives that were free spirits when it came to canine couplings. No arranged marriages for them, thank you very much. They chose their own partners from a huge and diverse gene pool, which is why you humans don't have a clue about most mongrels' heritage (and neither do we!). In comparison, pedigrees have been bred selectively, and this has meant they have been 'dogged' by genetic problems.

Bitsers

There is a certain aura of mystery about the unique and individual mongrel. We come in a huge assortment of shapes, colours, sizes and temperament (very friendly, friendly, and not quite so friendly). A bitser puppy is a furry surprise package, as indeed I was to prove to my humans, as documented in my biography, *A Tale of Two Puppies*. Snowy (a Terrier mix of small stature) was already part of the household, and my humans wanted a puppy that would grow to roughly the same size. The RSPCA suggested *moi*, an eight-week-old Foxie cross... or so they thought. My human picks up the story:

> In the puppy melee, our boy stood out as the best looking one there. With his shiny black coat, dappled grey socks, bat ears and cute little stump for a tail, we couldn't help but fall in love. When he joined us, Sox was three kilograms and two bricks high. He could walk under Snowy's tummy and fitted nicely on our laps. At 12 weeks, he had more than doubled his weight and by five months old

he was a piggy 16 kilograms. We were becoming more than a little suspicious that Sox had about as much foxy in him as we did. On his first birthday he weighed in at 25 kilograms. After countless enlargements to the doggy door, Sox's weight finally leveled at a hefty 30 kilograms. While his front half suggests a mixture of Cattle Dog and Kelpie, the rear end is Boxer with perhaps a dash of Doberman.

We mongrels may be banned from dog shows (brainless beauty pageants is a little harsh Snowy) but put us in agility or obedience competitions and watch us shine! Then there are the multitudes of other prestigious dog events which are dominated by mongrels. Aunty Boots won the biggest doggy smile at the local show and my boofy friend Bruno was champion tail waggler for two years running.

Bluebloods

In contrast to the uniqueness of the mongrel, purebreds do have a certain sameness about their appearance and temperament (yes, yes, Snowy, the term monotonous uniformity could be used). If you've seen one Golden Retriever, then you've seen 'em all. Of course, this is one of the main attractions of the pedigree. Some humans don't like surprises. They want the predictability of a certain breed to know exactly how their puppy will develop: height and weight, coat colour, tail length, even the amount of ear droop.

I feel a whine of concern when humans choose dogs based purely on the 'wow' factor, as mismatches make for some very unhappy relationships between dogs and humans. Unsuitability can mean a one-way trip to the animal refuge, and a pedigree as long as a Labrador's tail is no safeguard. There are thousands of purebreds 'doing time' simply because they didn't fit their human's lifestyle.

She was a lovely dog, apart from this funny habit of trying to round up my garden gnomes. (Miss Elderly, ex-owner of Lassie the Collie)

He was so energetic for a little dog. I wanted to watch TV. He wanted to go for walks. (Mr C. Potato, ex- owner of Toto the Jack Russell)

Poor little thing tried to keep up, but with those short legs and long hair, I had to keep carrying her home. Played havoc with my training times. (Mr Tri Athlete, ex-owner of Bella the Silky Terrier)

Then there is the sad case of the 'in vogue dogue'. Here I blame trendy TV shows, Hollywood blockbusters and brainless celebrities (Free Tinkerbell from the Blonde Bimbo is a great idea Snowy, but maybe the dog enjoys being an accessory.) Alas, the human is a fickle creature. Today's fashionable dog is tomorrow's forgotten cast-off, as thousands of spotty dogs discovered once the kerfuffle of *101 Dalmatians* died down.

The Australian National Kennel Council places all pedigree breeds within seven groups (no, boring and bland is not a group, Snow). Rather than list the characteristics of each (tedious and not fit for a dog-authored book such as this), I have opted for the World Domination Rating (WDR), a fun 'tongue in muzzle' look at each group's temperament. Use it wisely to help select your perfect dog buddy.

....

Sox's World Domination Rating

Toy dogs (WDR 9/10)
Chihuahuas, Pugs, Maltese, Pomeranians
Possesses the brains and motivation, but lacks credibility.
'World domination is mine… if only I could ditch this sequined tutu.'

Terriers (WDR 8/10)

Jack Russells, Fox Terriers, Australian Terriers

Possesses the energy and confidence, but can never stop still long enough to plan.

'Yes, of course I want to rule the world, just so busy with ball chasing, hole digging, rat patrol, the cat next door...'

Working (WDR 7/10)

Cattle Dogs, Kelpies, Collies

Possesses more than enough intelligence, but gets sidetracked easily.

'World ascendancy? Not a problem. I'll attend to it, just after I've rounded up these last few sheep.'

Gundogs (WDR 6/10)

Setters, Pointers, Spaniels, Retrievers

Possesses the stamina, but has trouble focusing on the bigger picture.

'Yep, I'm in, but'... stop...point...quiver... 'only if it involves guns and water.'

Hounds (WDR 5/10)

Bloodhounds, Basset Hounds, Beagles

Possesses the endurance but lacks leadership skills.

'Be onto the total world control thingy, straight after my buddies and I follow up on this scent.'

Utility (WDR 4/10)

Akitas, Schnauzers, Boxers, Rottweilers, Dobermans

Possesses the brawn, but lacks creativity.

'Huh, me in charge of everything? So whadda I do to make it happen?'

Non-sporting (WDR 3/10)

Poodles, Dalmatians, Keeshonds

Possesses the charisma, but lacks the killer instinct.

'World domination? My pleasure, straight after din dins and a good lie down'.

....

Decisions, decisions

Despite what some celebrities believe, dogs aren't fashion accessories. The best dog is not the one that matches your coat, hat or handbag, but one that matches your lifestyle. Before you fall for the big brown eyes and the fluffy coat, give yourself a critical appraisal. Be honest now and no cheating. If you think sweating is uncouth and your idea of a workout is picking up the remote, choose a dog that can share your sofa and your indolent ways. Conversely, hyperactive types need a dog that can keep them company on the daily marathons. Find your 'perfect fit' dog and you have a companion for life.

I began the chapter by presenting the great bitser/ blueblood conundrum. Of course, like all philosophical puzzles, there is no answer. Nor should there be. Regardless of all the hoopla and snobbery, the passions and beliefs, all dogs—bitsers, bluebloods and every combination in between—are descendents of Mr and Ms Wolf (*Canis lupus*). We share a common heritage and a common need: a forever family in an always home.

The dog is always the best animal.

The Human Perspective on Choosing the Right Dog for You

Sox knows his stuff here, his 'paws for thought' is spot on. The beauty of a dog is really in their personality and temperament, not their looks. There have been cases where the breeding of purebred dogs has gone horribly wrong because of indiscriminate breeding that focused more on the aesthetic appeal of the dogs rather than on good temperament or sound health. This has resulted in genetic faults from in-breeding. So if you're looking at a purebred puppy or dog, always select one from a reputable breeder or animal welfare shelter where they have been checked by a vet and temperament tested.

Over the years some breeds have become extremely popular due to their appearance in a movie. The Dalmatian is an ideal example. After *101 Dalmatians*, the breed's popularity soared and it wasn't long before animal shelters began to bulge at the seams with black-and-white spotted dogs. This caused the Dalmatian Breeders Association to come up with a slogan, '101 reasons why you should not buy a Dalmatian'. The campaign was designed to encourage people to think carefully before choosing the Dalmatian.

The Dalmatian is an attractive dog, but they are very strong willed and not for everyone. Dogs that appear in movies undergo months and months of training. Film producers often use many dogs to achieve the results they want. What you see up there on the screen is not just one well-behaved, easily trained dog, but the result of a lot of hard work and editing. So do your homework before selecting the breed that is right for you. Research their personality and breed traits. You might look at two or three breeds, especially if you plan to acquire a mixed breed.

Also, it makes good sense to meet the puppy's parents, if possible. The rationale here is that they will more than likely have the personality and stamina of at least one of their parents. Always try to match your puppy to your own personality and lifestyle. It's pointless to select a large boisterous breed if you don't have an active lifestyle or you have limited space or time to devote to them. Don't select by emotion alone.

Indy's Washing-day blues

A classic case of a dog not having their needs met was Indy, a one-year-old German Shepherd that was pulling washing off the line. When Bark Busters were called in they found Indy in a concrete yard devoid of anything other than a large kennel in one corner and a rotary clothesline in the other.

It was obvious that Indy's needs were not being met and that she had no alternative than to entertain herself by pulling washing off the line. The therapist spent a lot of time explaining to the owners that they had failed to provide Indy with one of the four basic needs: entertainment.

She suggested that they provide Indy with some interactive toys, such as a Buster Cube or Play and Learn toys that encourage dogs to use their mind and would give her hours of fun, taking her focus off the clothesline.

Bark Busters say:

• Pick a puppy or dog that approaches you freely.

• Look for the ones that sit quietly and are easily controlled.

• Avoid the puppy/dog that wriggles around, shows no interest in humans and tries to use its mouth to get away.

• Never pick the puppy or dog that runs away or barks at you.

• Think about adopting a puppy or dog from an animal welfare shelter where they will have been vet checked and temperament tested for you.

3 Getting Started

🐾 Sox's paws for thought

Dogs – value humans over possessions
Humans – value possessions over dogs

The puppy (or older dog) of your dreams is sitting adoringly at your feet, gazing up with an air of expectation. If you are a random, disorganised sort of human, this could be one of those awkward 'oh no, I haven't got anything for my new companion, not even a collar' moments. Or you could be a well-planned individual, who leaves nothing to chance. You want to get everything your new canine chum will need, before she arrives Well, you are both in luck. I am here to help with all those difficult accessorising decisions, because no-one knows what the well-pawed dog around town needs better than the four-legged philosopher.

Puppy/dog essentials

One loving, patient and responsible human—by far the most important thing. Don't underestimate how much patience and time you'll need, particularly with a new pup. They might be cute, but they're a lot of work. The road ahead is fraught with wee accidents, unfortunate deposits, chewed shoes and scratched mats—you have been warned.

Collar

There's an endless selection of collars available, from the ordinary to the eclectic (the purple feathery thing encased in diamantes). Ignore all this nonsense from certain quarters about collars being shackles of canine bondage (that means you, Bluey, from the militant Canine Workers Union). Dogs don't really mind wearing them. Just take it slowly with a puppy. You don't want to rush the whole thing and make them collar shy. Factor in some 'getting to know you' time, when they can sniff, play and even have a nibble of the collar. Next, try putting the collar on for short periods of time. Then the pup can have a go! (Sorry, couldn't resist the old human collar joke.) Don't forget puppies grow quickly, so check the fit regularly. If there's even a sniff of a too-tight collar, Blue and his cronies will be knocking at your door and demanding collar compensation.

Being dogs of senior years, Snowy and I have seen our share of collars. My personal favourite is my current one: a rakish little black model, adorned with razzle dazzle silver bones (proving I am not against bling *per se*). This one came to me when I accidentally lunged at a cat and snapped my old collar completely through. As it happened at the vet, a neck-naked dog was not exactly *de rigueur*, and a collar was quickly purchased. Snow has a very ordinary cotton collar, but has a secret desire for a black leather studded number (small dog syndrome?).

Identification tag

Yes, most clever puppies do know where they live, but we sometimes need human help to get home. Don't forget to microchip us too, tags can fall off and get lost. (I have a weakness for those bone shaped tags—kitsch but cute.)

Lead

Introduce a lead to your puppy gradually, the same way as the collar. Be slow, steady and patient. Puppies are clever little devils and it won't take long before they make the connection between that length of cotton and walkies. Why, they'll think the lead is the dog's whiskers in no time.

Snowy uses a retractable lead. Being a free spirit (read untrainable Terrier) she likes to roam far and wide on her walkies. This type of lead gives her the illusion of independence, but still keeps her safe. Her lead is a perfect example of getting what you pay for. Initially, our humans went for the 'cheap and nasty', which worked well until Snowy caught sight of a juicy tabby (was it one or two minutes into the walk?). The next lead was much more expensive, but has survived countless attempted cat assaults and is still going strong after eight years.

Bed or basket

No, your bed is not appropriate. Be strong. You are the alpha human, remember. No use folding at the first plaintive puppy whimper. We need our own dedicated doggy divan. A dog's bed is not just a place to sleep. It is our haven from the madding world, a place for retreat and contemplation. As with collars and leads, the bed connoisseur is spoilt for choice.

To ensure you let your sleeping dogs lie, here are Sox's Top Tips.

- Baskets are good for the non-chewing canine, so best kept away from young mouths.

  I loved my basket. It was so tasty and really helped with my teething.
  (Jaws the Pup)

- Tent beds are snug and cosy, popular with those bitten by the nesting urge.

- Hammock beds are perfect for keeping young and old bones off cold floors. Please buy one that can hold your dog's weight. My psyche is still very fragile after that embarrassing incident.

- Bedding material and pillows need careful thought. They should be washable (lots of puppy wee on the horizon, remember) and robust. The old cushion did add an exotic

Middle Eastern feel to our boudoir, until Snowy discovered it was more fun as a toy. Surprising just how far feathers float.

- Beds also double as secure storage areas. I have tucked a range of precious items in my bed for later consumption. You humans really do need to develop an appreciation of an aged bone, or twice buried piece of sausage.

- One bed is sufficient for most, unless their name is Snowy.

Food and water bowls

Stainless steel or ceramic are best, and should be sturdy enough to last the distance. Puppies have sharp teeth and know how to use them!

Coats

What's hanging in my wardrobe? Not much, to be honest. I am a thick-coated (and thick- skinned) dog and don't feel the cold very much. This means coats aren't really on my radar (or my back, thankfully). Before you buy a coat for your impressionable and easily embarrassed young pup, ask yourself whether it's necessary for warmth, or simply a fashion item. Obviously, for some dogs with thin (mangy?) fur, a coat is an essential item for winter wear. I do find that doggy coats bring out some strong emotions in canines. A definite 'love 'em or hate 'em' item.

> In that silly tartan coat I looked like an overweight tea cosy with legs and was the laughing stock of the whole street. It was 'lost' in no time. (S-x, friend of Snowy)

> That pink woolen number with matching ribbons was completely at odds with the chic and stylish canine I am. (S---y, friend of Sox)

> I love my coat. It keeps me warm and snug. (Fifi Furhound the Poodle, no friend of Sox or Snowy)

The great outdoors

Dogs love the great outdoors, and no canine household is complete without these important inclusions:

Doggy door

If you think these things are unnecessary, let me mention two words: puppy bladder. This piece of doggy anatomy may be small, but it is super efficient. In a few short tail wags, water can miraculously be transformed into liquid gold. And if you don't want this liquid to anoint your house, there are two choices: get interrupted constantly or install a doggy door. Case closed.

A doggy door is something my kennel mate and I highly recommend. It allows us to come and go as we like, without bothering our humans. If we need an urgent leg lift, fancy a midnight bone gnaw, or want to investigate those strange night time noises, we can. Please get a door large enough to accommodate any future increase in doggy girth size. (Note to self: lay off the chicken wings until door is enlarged again.)

Fence

A fence is an essential requirement to keep your puppy in and others out. Dogs are nosey parkers and enjoy gazing beyond our dogmain to the outside world, so a see-through fence would be appreciated. Some Houdini's enjoy going over, under and occasionally through the fence. While there can be good reasons for this behaviour (the cute bitch down the road, loneliness, to get the postie) some dogs are simply bitten by wanderlust. Ask why and the response may be 'Why not?' Whenever the fence subject is raised, Snowy likes to bang on about how, as a 'petite puppy' she could squeeze through the slats to the exciting world beyond. She makes out it was clever and calculated, but I'm sure it was good luck. Anyway, the days of squeezing that body through anything are long gone.

Toys

We need dedicated dog toys, not human cast-offs. The four-legged philosopher knows the difference between a Jimmy Choo and an old shoe, but does your average pup? Best to play safe and give them specific pooch playthings. My all time favourites are soccer ball, Frisbee, tennis ball, squeak bone, ball-on-a-rope, rope pull, rawhide ball, rubber bone, throw ball, rubber ring …oh, and did I mention balls?

Toileting trials and tribulations

(Forgive my alliteration, it was simply too good to pass up).

As I have already broached the sensitive issue of puppy bladders, it seems appropriate to mention the terrible Ts— toilet training. House training your puppy (I shall call him Mr X because I can) is all about getting the timing right. Indeed, the question is not so much to pee, or not to pee, but when to do the deed. Observe Mr X closely when he is inside. Sniffing with intent usually precedes rear end action. Take him straight outside, for a pup's bladder and bowel waits for no human. Mr X also needs a quick visit to the lawn after he has eaten and slept. These are classic toilet times.

Don't forget lots of praise if things are forthcoming, but make it original. 'Good dog' is so yesterday. Newspaper makes a great port-a-loo and protects your precious floor. Choose something interesting, thanks, and keep the tabloids for the kittens. Expect plenty of mishaps, so please be patient and understanding. Rubbing noses in mistakes? *Grrrrrr!* My hackles are bristling at the thought of such barbarity.

To be frank, these memories of my puppyhood are rather hazy, but my human assures me there is nothing in my past which would cause embarrassment. Apparently I was a textbook trainee and had the pee protocol licked in two shakes of a Terrier's tail. Would you expect any less of the Philosophical Pooch, even in his tender years? Others dogs, that shall remain nameless, took much longer to train, and even now are a little lax in minding their Pee's and Q's.

Unwelcome accessories

These items are also known in dog circles as 'howler ware'. That's 'howler' as in 'a glaring and ludicrous blunder'. Any self-respecting dog with taste (that cuts out Poodles, Samoyeds and Rottweilers) would run a mile when confronted with a dress, T shirt, beret or indeed any designer doggy item that has no practical application. Some humans have difficulty remembering we are living animals, not toys, fashion accessories, dolls, babies, children or indeed any small version of *Homo sapiens*. Call me a fashion philistine, but below are my pet hates in howler ware:

- Dog prams, strollers or carriers–that's what legs do and we have four of them.
- Shawls–acceptable for elderly humans, not dogs.
- Bandanas–acceptable for motorbike-riding humans, not dogs.
- Bow ties–not acceptable for any species.
- Shoes, booties or any paw wear–acceptable for dogs working or walking in extreme conditions (snow, ice, broken glass); otherwise let our paws run free.
- Nappies–shocking but true, dog diapers really exist.

Snowy wants everyone to know her pet hates are cats, followed closely by mice. Let's not forget she IS a Terrier, after all.

You don't need to spend a fortune outfitting your pooch. We aren't into hound couture, so make it simple. Keep the expensive jewellery, designer shoes and silk scarves for the (human) ones you love (they can have the purple feathery thing encased in diamantes too!). The best accessory any dog can have is a loving human with great taste in dogs, just like I have.

Clothes don't maketh the dog.

The Human Perspective on Dog Essentials

Having Sox's input provides a rare glimpse into a dog's views on accessories. When Bark Busters is called in to train dogs or solve behavioural problems, we find that not surprisingly, some people can be confused as to what are the best accessories or equipment for their dogs. Or as Sox has mentioned, when owners anthropomorphise their dogs, believing they are little humans on four legs and treating them as substitute children, they can go overboard in the accessory department.

I totally agree with Sox in that above all else, dogs need a responsible, fair and reasonable human who can provide them with strong leadership. Lack of leadership is at the root of all behavioural problems, and without leadership a dog may display fear, anxiety or aggression. This need for leadership is strong in every dog's psyche and some dogs have been known to literally swap owners, moving in with the people next door or up the road, just to be with a human who has the skills they need to feel secure and safe.

Dog essentials

Collars are an essential accessory, and all dogs should have a well-fitted collar that is checked for comfort regularly, as well as an identity disc with relevant contact details. Our research and training experience has identified that the best collars are those made of natural, not synthetic materials. Collars made from synthetic fibre will conduct static electricity and may be uncomfortable, causing some dogs to constantly scratch at their collars.

These collars can cause problems for the human and dog relationship too, especially when the human walks across a synthetic fibre carpet to pat their dog, and instead of a loving pat both dog and human receive an electric shock.

Dogs don't really care which lead you use as long as they get to go for a walk. When it comes to the human's comfort, the best material for a lead is cotton. Cotton offers strength as well as gentleness to the hand holding it, without any risk of burning.

Sox knows full well that dogs need their own bed and private space to feel secure and safe. If ever we find a case of aggression in a household, generally the owners have failed to provide their dog with his own bed.

Coats

Bark Busters don't have an opinion one way or the other on dog coats. However we are mindful that dogs do have a natural coat that adjusts naturally to changes in climate. When it gets cold a dog's coat will bulk up, and will shed when the temperature begins to climb. It may be necessary to provide a coat if a dog is sick, ageing or extremely short coated.

Doggy doors

Dogs need lots of fresh air, exercise and sunshine so a doggy door is an important fixture and one we at Bark Busters recommend to a lot of our clients. It can prevent some behavioural problems and offers dog owners the assurance that they're providing their pet with the best of both worlds.

Fences

Some people mistakenly believe that to keep your dog confined is cruel. I can honestly tell you that anyone who allows their dog to roam freely is irresponsible, and is placing their dog's welfare at risk. It is akin to allowing a two-year-old out of the house alone. Dogs don't have a conscience—they need human guidance to teach them right from wrong to ensure that they turn into a well-adjusted animal.

Reckless Ruby

Ruby, an Irish setter, was the much-loved pet of Dave and Hilda who wanted her to have everything her heart desired. They believed that Ruby's behavioural problems were due to confinement, and felt that keeping such a beautiful creature locked up was cruel, especially a dog bred for hunting.

So one day they gave her the freedom they thought she deserved. They opened their front gate and let her run free. That afternoon Ruby was hit by a car while chasing a cat across a busy highway. Luckily for Dave and Hilda she survived the accident. They then called Bark Busters in to help solve her behavioural problems. We didn't have to work too hard at explaining to them the error of their ways.

Bark Busters say:

- Dogs naturally seek leadership and need it to feel secure and safe. If the human does not provide it, behavioural problems can surface.

- The best collar is one made from natural fibres. The best lead is one made of cotton; it will be softer on hands and won't cause any burning of skin.

- Coats are okay but more suitable for aged, ailing or extremely short-coated dogs. A dog's natural coat will adjust to changes in climate.

- Doggy doors are a great idea; they prevent some behavioural problems and allow dogs to enjoy the best of both worlds.

- Fences are a must. Dogs should be confined at all times for their own protection.

- Beds are vitally important to a dog's welfare. Without a space of their own, a dog may develop behaviour problems. The type of bed is irrelevant as long as it provides warmth and proper support.

4 Canine Communication

🐾 Sox's paws for thought

Dogs – communicate using body language
Humans – communicate using verbal language

In some ways, this chapter could have been *Numero Uno*, as communicating effectively with your dog is what it's all about. Get that part right and many dog behaviour problems simply won't exist. The biggest impediment to open and effective communication is fairly obvious: we speak dog and you speak human and never the twain shall meet.

As there are very few truly bilingual humans among you (my co-author being one), the trick is to get some meaningful dialogue (or dogalogue, if you'll excuse the paw pun) happening by communicating in other ways. Think outside the kennel and be creative. If you aren't the lateral type, my suggestions should help pave the way to a long and happy relationship with your dog.

Remember, we are really wolves (yes, even your teensy weensy Chloe—hard to believe I know) in domesticated doggy clothing, and are happiest in a situations which reflect how our ancestors lived. With this in mind, keep the two 'p' words up front when dealing with dogs: pack and position. Dogs are social animals that like to live in groups. Everything we do revolves around our pack and the position we hold.

While all dogs are born equal, some are most definitely more equal than others. This is where you, the significant human in our life, steps up to the bowl (we hope). Social democracy, egalitarianism, equal opportunities—what a dog's breakfast! We don't want a bar of that nonsense. Granted, there is the odd trouble-making canine. Bluey, representing the militant Canine Workers Union (CWU) tried to make waves, but his list of grievances (ergonomically designed kennels, weekends off, bone allowance, smaller herds) got short shift from the general dog population.

We want a clear hierarchy, headed by a strong, but fair alpha wolf—our esteemed leader. Want to take a crazy guess at who that leader should be? If you knew immediately I meant YOU, then congratulations, you probably have the leadership qualities we are looking for. If you were unsure, then the position as alpha human may not suit. Weak leaders make for confused and unhappy pack members. Forget dogs and consider keeping the innocuous guinea pig, or perhaps those *vive la revolution* rodents, the rats.

Hopefully I have scared away the weak and feeble, and can now turn my attentions to you, the potential new alpha human of the pack. So how do you command your motley crew without the gift of dog-speak? Before you can develop your communication skills, it's important to understand the main difference between the species: humans rely heavily on speech, dogs on body language. Following is a sweeping generalisation about the human race, so if you are easily offended, you may prefer to skip this part.

Humans are very verbal, but I do wonder how much of the yakkity yak stuff actually constitutes real communication. How often are messages mixed up? You often say one thing, but your body clearly means something quite different. In contrast, we canines really do wear our hearts on our sleeves—well our whole bodies really. Our feelings are open and obvious, with no hidden agendas. With dogs, what you see is what you get—so why do so many humans not 'get it'?

My humans kept picking up my bones, but not my warnings. How could they miss the message, it was as plain as the nose on my bared muzzle? It's not my fault things got ugly. (The Bone Bitch)

I didn't want another ride. I hate cars. I thought that had been made quite clear. But no, they had to drag me in straight after dinner. I make no apologies for what I left on the back seat. (Bill Yus the Basenji)

It's not all doom and gloom however. Sometimes the planets align and this whole communication conundrum works out:

Well obviously I'm proud, but it isn't the award or all the attention. What I'm most pleased about is that I could alert my family to the danger. The rule has always been 'never wake a sleeping adult', but I knew this was an emergency and called for a break in protocol. Just lucky they realised I wasn't being annoying. (Lassie the Twelfth–Dog Hero)

Our stupendous senses

We dogs use our senses to help us understand the world around us and interact with other canines. Let's take a peek at these in more detail because knowledge is power when it comes to the world of dogs. If you want to maintain that alpha position and be able to train your dog effectively, communication is the key.

Voice

While dogs are very much body-oriented communicators, this doesn't mean we are mutes (mutts, yes, mutes, no). Indeed, we have a rich and varied range of vocalisations, depending on the situation. Barking, whining and howling can express many different emotions: happiness, excitement, frustration or boredom, although I would caution against trying to vocalise like a dog. There are subtle nuances that could easily offend: a bark with the wrong intonation could prove embarrassing. It's hard to misconstrue the meaning of a growl, however, and this is an effective way of letting your dog know you are unhappy (just check the neighbours aren't close when you let loose).

Sight

Thanks to our wild ancestors, we have excellent sight and night vision (hard to bring down that deer if you can't see in front of your nose). This means the movement of small creatures in the grass, the passing car and the stranger are all worthy of attention. It also means we make great night watch dogs. Being such observant creatures, hand signals can work a treat in training. On the topic of eyes, staring competitions are seen by dogs as highly dominant behaviour. Use with caution around dogs like Agro Arnie. He could take it as a challenge.

Occasionally our eyesight lets us down, as Snowy can attest. Granted our male human didn't look familiar in the bike helmet, but fancy bailing him up like that. I haven't let her forget that embarrassing indiscretion—and yes, it has made it into the book, Snow.

Hearing

Regardless of the size or shape, dogs' ears are highly efficient. We have acute hearing and can detect noises with a much higher frequency than humans (squeaky toys, squeaky cats and squeaky mice). While this is what makes us such efficient guard dogs, it also means we are easily distracted by extraneous noises when training, so keep this in mind.

Smell

The super pooch powers just keep getting better. Our amazing sense of smell, combined with the canine food obsession, means that liver treat in your back pocket is going to get our attention like nothing else. Use it wisely in training and you will have us eating out of your fingers.

Touch

OK, so this is one area of sense that you lot win hands (and opposable thumbs) down. Although many humans use touch (patting and stroking) as a training reward, most dogs, given the choice, would go for a tasty tidbit or their favourite squeaky toy. On the touch subject, please never use physical punishment on your dog. This doesn't help us learn, it simply makes us fearful and resentful.

How to be the alpha human your dog dreams about

- Walk tall and confidently.
- Eat before your dog (but don't forget to feed us).
- Be strong and enforce rules.
- Don't be a pushover, but be fair.
- Don't chase after dogs that won't come to you (it's so demeaning).
- Growl to show you are unhappy.
- Never use physical punishment.

Remember, dogs are a package deal. It's not just the body, ear or tail language you have to read. I agree our tails (or stubs) are very expressive, but do not judge a dog by tail alone. To assist those humans who are dog-language illiterates, here are some purely fictional canine characters with very telling body signs:

Submissive Snowy – needs a soft and gentle approach

- crouches down or rolls onto back
- tail tucked between legs
- ears flattened
- eyes downcast
- licking lips apprehensively
- may present appeasement wee

Playful Patch – happy and confident

• body relaxed or in play bow position
• tail wagging
• ears up
• eyes happy

Fearful Fred – take it slow and easy

• crouches down or cowers
• tail tucked between legs
• ears flattened
• eyes fearful and watching
• teeth bared

Agro Arnie – red alert

• standing up
• tail stiff and upright
• ears forward
• full eye contact
• legs stiff
• teeth bared
• hackles up

As alpha human you have a great responsibility to the members of your pack, be it one or one hundred. Use your power wisely and fairly. Remember *noblesse oblige*: with privilege and position come duty and care for those you control.

We have two ears and one tail, that we may listen the more and wag the less.

The Human Perspective on Body Language

There is much speculation about how much dogs actually comprehend when it comes to human language. One thing we know for sure is that dogs speak 'dog language'—it is based on body language and guttural sounds and is one that all dogs understand. A dog living with an English or French-speaking family could easily communicate with a dog living with a family who only spoke Japanese. This is because dogs have a universal language that has no geographical barriers.

Problems occur when the human over-complicates communication with copious amounts of dialogue that just serves to confuse the dog. How often do you see a dog turning his head from side to side trying to understand what the human is saying?

A common mistake we see is where the owner believes that their dog is stupid or stubborn because he fails to follow instructions. Dogs are neither stubborn nor stupid; they are pack animals that need human leadership. The best and easiest way to communicate with your dog is to keep it simple.

Training is most effectively accomplished when you give your dog a command in a normal speaking voice using simple, single words, followed by a one growled word correction, followed quickly by praise and encouragement. All dogs respond to high-pitched melodious tones. Don't lose your patience, and never ever hit your dog. Hands are only for patting.

How to read a dog's body language

You'll find it easier to communicate with your dog if you look to see what he's trying to tell you. Dogs use their bodies to relay to other dogs what they're feeling. All 'down or lowered' body language is submissive; 'up' is assertive and confident.

A dog that lowers his height when corrected shows that he has complete respect for you. It is then time for you to acknowledge his submission with praise. However, if a dog retains his height, and his body messages are unchanged, he's saying that your correction was totally ineffectual and you have not yet gained his complete respect.

Unlike humans, who can display body language in total contradiction to what they are saying, dogs unashamedly show their true feelings through their body movements and ear and tail placement. If they're feeling frightened, they will lower their height, tuck their tail way down or between their legs, and will endeavour to make themselves appear smaller, relaying subliminal messages that they are no threat to anyone. Or they may raise their hackles in aggression to repel the object of their fear. When they're feeling comfortable, they will appear happy, unafraid of pulling themselves up to their full height, ears forward and tail way up high, able to take on the world.

Last-chance Billy

Billy, a 12-month-old crossbred Cattle Dog—the long-suffering pet of a busy executive couple—was given his last chance to prove he could obey his owners' orders. When we were called in, we were told that this was Billy's last chance. His owners had run out of patience and he had to step up to the mark and shape up or ship out.

This surprised us as we felt that Billy was getting a raw deal. So we set about explaining to the owners in the nicest possible way that Billy was not a bad dog, he was just a misunderstood dog that couldn't comprehend what they were trying to tell him.

We showed the owners how to communicate by using a normal speaking voice when asking Billy to do something and when showing and guiding him, and by using a low-pitched voice when correcting. He quickly caught on. Billy was one of the most intelligent dogs we had ever met; he just needed someone to speak 'dog' to him.

Bark Busters say:

- Dogs show their feelings through body language, so look at your dog's body movements, as well as his tail and ear placement, to see what he's trying to tell you.

- Dogs don't speak English, French or Japanese—they speak 'dog'.

- Communicating with your dog is easy—just keep it simple and you'll see immediate results.

- Use a normal speaking voice when asking your dog to do something, followed by a low-voice tone correction and high-pitched praise.

- Dogs have many amazing senses, but their sense of smell will override all else.

- Hands are for patting. Don't ever smack your dog; this will only breed mistrust.

5 Bon Appétit

🐾 Sox's paws for thought

Dogs – eat to live
Humans – live to eat

Ah, the food chapter, one of my favourite topics and something to really get my teeth into. In this I am not alone. Feed time is an important part of every dog's life. This can be traced back to our wild ancestors when food wasn't just an interesting diversion, but deadly serious. The pack's survival depended on making a kill. Move forward a few thousand years and we still take our dinner seriously. It may be more a case of waiting for the can to be opened than stalking prey, but try taking our bowl away and see what happens.

Would Sir like to order...?

Which type of commercial dog food is best for your furry friend? As a connoisseur of fine food and drink, I volunteered my time, tongue and tummy to this important research. It was hard work, but some dog had to do it. I sampled the food from cheap eats to fine dining, and my words of wisdom are quite simply don't be tricked into false economy and think that buying the cheap version is the best option for your dog or your wallet. I know some dogs that are prima donnas when it comes to their tummies. No use buying a tonne of the dry stuff if Miss Prissy won't touch it. Then your kind-hearted and ever faithful other dog would be forced to eat the 'tasteless cardboard' for months.

Here are some pros and cons of the various types of commercial dog foods available:

Dry

- Value for money, but somewhat lacking in aroma and flavour.
- Crunchy texture helps to keep teeth clean.
- Easy to store (unless you have hungry rodents and a deaf Terrier on guard).
- Can come in cute little bone shapes.

Semi-moist

- Medium cost, but has unusual consistency and flavour.
- Safe from marauding rodents, so it's easy to store.

Canned

- Most expensive, but it's definitely the yummiest.
- Easy to eat.
- Needs to be refrigerated once open.
- Safe from marauding rodents.

Regardless of what type you choose, please buy the best-quality dog food you can afford. Remember, we dogs are what we eat. This brings me to Snowy the epicurean and her findings. Apparently she liked the 'canned cat' the best. When I pointed out her favourite delight was actually made FOR cats, not FROM cats, she was shocked. Terriers, eh?

For a while, our human got the self-sufficiency bug and decided to cook up our dinner, a healthy combination of chicken mince, rice, carrots and peas. Not that we minded. The aroma of the stewing chicken was superb. Really got my digestive juices and slobber glands flowing. The stuff tasted pretty good too. Our days of home-cooked goodies were numbered, however. After we performed a particularly enthusiastic double dog drool act, our human slipped in the dribble. Next thing we knew she was whistling the latest dog food jingles and our home-cooked goodies were only memories. Which brings me to an important point: if you decide to change our food, please do it slowly. Upset pooch tummies are unpleasant for all members of the family, but particularly the dog.

Table scraps are also known in the canine world as the ambrosia from above. Oh, chop fat, burnt sausage, pie crust... I am powerless before your magnificence. There's no denying we dogs appreciate human food, probably even more than you do, which makes it so unfair that it's off limits. Oh, I know, it's too fatty, too salty, too sugary, which, in a sad twist of perversity, is exactly why it tastes so good. Anyway, no use whining over lost food opportunities. Too much is bad for dogs and that's that.

Bones

The great bone debate is contentious, but I managed to dig up these two important points: raw bones good, cooked bones bad. Raw bones help with our dental hygiene. All that chewing, munching and gnawing keeps our teeth and gums in tip top condition. Please don't complain about a dog's bone breath. It may not be the fresh minty smell so admired by humans, but it is preferable to rotten teeth. Raw bones also offer some nutritional value in the form of calcium, vitamins and minerals. Finally, raw bones are the perfect snack to give us because we love 'em— some dogs a bit too much.

Sundays and Wednesdays are our 'chicken tonight' evenings. I'm a thigh dog, but Snow prefers the wings. Chicken bones are the 'here and now' and disappear down our throats in no time. We also indulge in the larger beef bones once a week. These keep us occupied for hours on end, tearing and worrying away any flesh. Once stripped, they get buried for later and can even be used as a toy (a multi-functioned bone, indeed). Snow and I have whiled away many happy hours playing bone catchy. Unfortunately, there is too much of a good thing when it comes to bones. Recently I suffered from bloated bone belly due to the excesses of the night before.

And now we come to one of life's biggest disappointments: the curse of the cooked bone. The scent of a roasting leg of lamb can almost drive a dog to madness. Alas, this delicacy is brittle, can splinter, cause throat and digestive problems, and will always be a forbidden fruit.

Feeding frequency

Some dog gurus suggest feeding dogs twice a day, especially smaller breeds with correspondingly smaller tummies. Others say once is enough. Dogs are, naturally, a little emotive over this issue:

Three times a day is best. I use up a lot of energy. (Benji the Jack Russell Terrier)

I could probably worry down a few mouthfuls a couple of times a week. (Anna Rexic)

I like my din dins in 10 servings spread across the day, 'cos I'm on a diet. (Sam the Labrador)

As often as I want. (A Doberman name withheld on request)

Twice a day, most definitely. If your mean-spirited human doesn't offer breakfast, do a bit of forward planning and leave a little aside from dinner. NB: Keep away from hungry and much larger kennel mate. (Snowy, President of the Pooch Pro-Breakfast Movement)

I have a 'delicate constitution' and was plagued by stomach upsets and wind, until my humans changed from feeding me one big meal to three smaller meals per day. Now I'm much happier and my humans are too. (Greed E. Guts the Poodle)

I'm a once a day dog, myself, which is why late afternoon is by far my favourite time. After a vigorous game of ball chasing and a brisk walk, we rest on the grass. As evening settles it's time for DIN DINS. After wolfing down our food, Snow and I undertake the time-honoured dog tradition: 'exchanging of the bowls'. Another dog's dinner bowl is always more interesting than one's own. Tuckered out and with a full belly, it's straight off to nod nod land for this big black dog.

And to drink...?

Water is the drink of choice of lions and wolves, so it must be good. I like my H_2O straight from the tap, with that delicious undertone of plastic hose. Snowy and I have two 'lap pools', just in case one springs a leak, is knocked over or runs out. It's surprising how much water we get through, especially in hot weather. Very occasionally, I might indulge in a drop of milk, shaken, not stirred.

Gastronomical delights in the backyard and beyond

The favourite backyard treat is the sump café; moonlight dining with a twist. You never know what treasures you'll find there, rancid fat, egg shell, bacon rind. Then there's the world of casual cuisine beyond the backyard. Some dogs eat grass for the nutrients and roughage. Others do it to assist a vomit. The four-legged philosopher does it because he likes it. A good grass chow-down on our walkies is hard to beat. The grass isn't always greener, but definitely tastier on the other side. Then there is manure munching. Although it gets a great reaction from humans, this isn't the reason we do it (promise). Cows and other herbivore waste is interesting stuff to sniff and the occasional poo fondue isn't going to harm us.

Poisonous pooch pickings

Contrary to what some Chihuahua owners believe, we are not small, furry humans. Many of the foods humans enjoy are toxic to dogs. Too much can even kill us. The main offenders are:

Chocolate—I have had a few illicit wrapper licks in my time, but nothing to equal Benji's overdose. It was a familiar scene for easy pickings—a child's birthday party—plenty of dropped cake and a vacuuming dog. He lived, but what a tummy ache!

Onions and garlic—These are insidious little devils, often sneaking a ride down a dog's throat on table scraps, a slice of pizza, a bit of leftover soup, a dollop of stew. Some dogs react badly to even a little bit, so play it safe. Put any leftovers in the bin, not our bowls.

Coffee—Darn, there goes my morning latte. Just kidding, can't say I know any dog that enjoys this poison, but it takes all sorts.

Avocado, grapes, raisins, sultanas, macadamia nuts—Shelly, the farm dog, enjoyed sneaking avocados off the trees and burying them until they ripened. Clever sort of pooch, just a pity his hobby landed him in hospital.

Regardless whether we are a *bon appétit* type or a basic bog-in mutt, the dinner bowl is of top importance to dogs. As bringing down a moose is no longer on our radars, we rely solely on humans to make the right choices to ensure we are happy and healthy hounds. And as any Jenny Craig or Weight Watchers member will know, what you want isn't necessarily what you need.

Life's too short to chew bad bones.

The Human Perspective on Feeding your Dog

The dog's diet should not be complicated. Like humans, dogs need certain nutrients, fibre and balance in their diet to remain healthy. However what you feed your dog, believe it or not, also has a huge bearing on their behaviour.

As Sox says, the dog's ancestors lived off the land—they chased and caught their food, hunting in packs—and they did not go to the fridge to open a can. Modern society has made things so much easier for the dog and their owners, but it has not altered the dog's dietary needs.

I feed my own dogs' only raw food: raw meaty bones, raw veggies, the odd raw egg, kelp and small amounts of fish oil or oily sardines. The raw bones provide calcium and nutrients, found in the marrow. This kind of feeding means that my dogs do far less droppings than dogs fed on canned and dry food, which means their bodies are able to utilise more of the food they take in. I believe this is the way nature intended. If you do feed bones, choose soft bones such as rib and mutton flaps and give only raw bones not cooked, providing plenty of fresh water. Be sure to make any diet change a gradual one.

The raw versus prepared, canned or packaged food debate rages on. Our recommendation is this: if you want what's best for your dog but cannot come at the raw food option or don't have the necessary time or knowledge to cook your own, then listen to what Sox is telling you. Choose a good quality packaged food, available from vets and pet shops. On the surface the top-quality brand might look like a dearer option when you compare the size of the bags, but it is far superior and does not contain the fillers and additives of the cheaper brands. This means that you don't need to feed anywhere near as much of the top-quality food to get the same nutritional value as the cheaper options.

Bark Busters research, both in Australia and overseas, has shown that food containing preservatives, food colourings and harmful additives can cause hyperactivity in dogs.

To add credence to what we are saying here and to help you determine which food is best for your dog, you need look no further than the extensive research which has shown that some children overreact to food containing colourings and preservatives.

We mention carbohydrates as one of the main culprits in contributing to hyperactivity in dogs because the body converts carbohydrate into sugar which equals energy. A dog that is already energetic or hyperactive will only become more so if fed on high levels of carbohydrates, it's that simple.

If you're still not sure and want further proof, just think about highly strung race horses and what they're fed that makes them that way: they are fed high levels of carbohydrates.

Bark Busters say:

- If you cannot feed naturally, then ensure you feed a balanced diet or opt for a high-quality packaged food.

- If your dog is hyperactive, avoid food that contains high levels of carbohydrates, colourings and harmful preservatives.

- Feed only raw soft bones NEVER cooked bones and always supply lots of fresh water.

- Introduce all dietary changes gradually.

6 Dogs Behaving Badly

🐾 Sox's paws for thought

Dogs – no means no
Humans – no means no, most of the time

Although the really meaty dog issues (barking, biting, digging and walking worries) are dealt with separately later in the book, there are, sadly, other behaviours that drive humans to distraction. Some humans blame the dogs entirely; others fervently believe 'there are no bad dogs, just bad humans'. As the four-legged philosopher, I try to adopt an impartial and fair minded view—more a case of sitting between, rather than on the fence (those palings are sharp on a canine's rump).

Certainly many dogs behave badly because they are bored or lack training, and this can be traced back to their humans. But blame is so negative and achieves nothing. Often there are mitigating circumstances on both sides. The very fact that you are reading *Dog Logic* suggests you do care about your canine companion. This lifts my spirits and gives me heart. To those with dogs who aren't reading this book, shame, shame, shame!

The parents among you will understand the importance of being consistent with discipline (dogs are like small humans in many ways, except we are generally furrier, cuter and cleaner). Rules are just that—rules. They are not open to negotiation or interpretation. No means no and off limits means exactly that, regardless of when, where, what or whom.

Dogs don't understand mixed messages, changing circumstances or subtle differences. Snoozing on the sofa was okay yesterday, yet today gets the big 'no no'. All so very confusing. The difference is your offspring can ask why—we must simply wonder at our human's strange ways. No wonder there are so many dogs behaving badly.

Table manners

In *Bon appétit*, I explained the close link between canines and our tummies, so it should be no surprise that this can cause issues, from the low-key dinner drooling, to begging and finally the more serious food stealing. In the ideal canine world, alpha humans eat first, then dogs. This hierarchy often gets muddled and we don't know whether we're Fido or Fifi, top dog or minor mutt. Even if we are fed last, many humans think it is okay for dogs to be near, beside and sometimes on (hang your head Mr Dusty 'I'm so Spoilt' Chihuahua) the dinner table. As Mr Pavlov discovered all those years ago, we dogs learn by association. I have extrapolated this further and come up with Sox's Law of Dribble:

Table + human + food + possible treat for dog = copious dribble

For some dogs, seeing and smelling human food is all too much, and the flood gates open. While the dog is welcome at the table, the drool generally isn't. Being close to the action also means lots of tasty tidbits (manna from heaven) which fall to our level and are quickly cleaned up by the hovering hound. Some don't wait for the food drop and show remarkable initiative:

> *I tried all the most popular moves: the paw lift, the head tilt, the soft whine (by far the least effective method) and the perennial tail wag. The beg won paws down. I haven't met a human who can ignore this brilliantly choreographed routine. Hit the big time today: half a sausage, a marinated chicken wing and some banana muffin.*

> *(Sneaky Snow)*

Lastly are the delicious delicacies, left out, in full view and sniff range. To steal or not to steal? What is a dog to do?

Sox's Simple Solutions

- Feeding hierarchy: humans first, dog second, other pets third, any other animals fourth, those of the feline persuasion, last.
- Table and tidbits don't mix (think of your dog's waist).
- If you have a first-class doggy dribbler, keep them outside at food time.
- To avoid food-related heists, put away tasty temptations. Out of sight (and smell) is out of mind.

Chewing problems

Contrary to popular human belief, chewing is not just a puppy past time. Many teen, adult and even elderly dogs enjoy a chow-down on the odd item. Puppies chew to explore their world and also to relieve the discomfort of teething. Some just keep the habit up as they get bigger. Pups are not terribly discriminating with their chomps of choice. Neither are some dogs and therein lies the problem—an old boot, the hose, a cup and even the kitchen sink. So, while most things are really quite chewable, not everything is really quite allowable. We need clear direction from our humans on which is which. Destruction thy name does not have to be dog. Give us alternative things to gnaw on and we'll be happy.

Sox's Simple Solutions

- Offer rawhide chews, bones and other pro-chew items.
- Don't store your favourite leather shoes next to our favourite toy chews. Cases of mistaken identity are common.

Furniture foibles

Lounges, sofas and beds are popular rest spots for dogs. And who can blame them? We all enjoy a bit of luxury when it comes to sleeping. As a hedonist from way back, I can't resist the lure of soft cushions and warm blankets. The difference is I have my own, which I most certainly do not share with my humans (they're lovely, but who knows where they've been?). Mutual furniture use between humans and dogs is fraught with problems. Allow us up on the bed and there could well be some ownership issues raising their toothy heads in the future. You may have paid for the queen size ensemble, but some dogs believe that possession is nine-tenths of the paw:

> *The youngest human's bed made the best nest. But then he started to cramp my style and when I defended my castle, they behaved as if I had been in the wrong. ('Bubba' Benji the Jack Russell)*

> *Initially I didn't mind. He was really cute curled up under the blankets. After a while though, he started to growl when I wanted to get into bed. Give some dogs an inch of bedclothes and they take a mile. (Benji's human)*

Sox's Simple Solutions

• Dog beds for dogs, human beds for humans.

• Share your furniture with your dog at your peril. Hire a good lawyer who specialises in furniture disputes.

Tail chasing

The old tail chasey routine, eh? Haven't I seen my share of this craziness in the neighbourhood. This is a self-perpetuating behaviour that's an easy one to spot, but not to solve. The culprits are usually stir-crazy Bull Terriers with too much time on their paws. Bored, lonely and manic, they have nothing to do but chase the ever-moving tail.

Sox's Simple Solutions

• As a stumpy tail that has put up with a lifetime of derision, I consider long tails to be overrated. Catching in doors, wagging in faces, knocking over food bowls and now being the cause of obsessive-compulsive behaviour, the question has to be asked, exactly what good are they? However, not being a vindictive dog, I won't suggest the obvious solution.

• If boredom is the cause, give your dog more exercise and mental stimulation.

Washing worries

This is another of the stir-crazy behaviours' exhibited by dogs 'bored in the burbs'. Before you get angry, see it from our point of view. We are a species bred for chasing and killing our food, as part of a pack. It is our natural genetic make-up. Yet, we are stuck in a tiny backyard all day, bored and alone. Is it any wonder the flapping sheets and dangling pants offer a tantalising escape from this monotony? Once we drag them to the ground, we can continue the fun with some shredding and tearing. For the really adventurous, this activity can be combined with digging so you can bury some pieces for later.

Sox's Simple Solutions

• Once again, you need to offer your dog some boredom busters, and soon: more exercise, a sandpit, toys, perhaps even another canine companion.

• What about separating the dog and the washing? Maybe keep the washing inside while the dog is on the line…no, sorry, the other way round.

Escape artists

Some dogs just aren't happy behind a fence and seem to have a pathological need to get to the other side. They scrabble, scramble, leap and dig until they're free. But freedom is short lived. Along comes you-know-who with his dog-catching apparatus and these family pets suddenly become pound hounds. Humans despair if they have an escape artist and this is a common reason for surrendering four-legged friends to the shelter. Of course, as recidivist escapees, their chances of being successfully re-homed are low. Let's look at what can be done about the escaping dog, before it gets to the shelter stage.

Sox's Simple Solutions

- Spend quality time with your dog to find out why he's escaping. He could be bored and lonely, scared of noises and storms, or simply have the wanderlust. Don't take this as a canine vote of no confidence in you, the alpha human. Oh, and don't ask the dog. They won't tell.

- Once you know the cause, fill the need. Fido bored and lonely? Make the backyard a more interesting place than the big, bad world outside. Exercise him more. Offer some light entertainment to while away the hours like chews and play toys. Yes, a plasma TV would be lovely, Snowy, but it's hardly an essential.

- If all else fails, pooch-proof the enclosure. Put your fence on steroids. Make it taller, higher, bigger and all round better. Change from wire (too much paw purchase) to brick or timber. Fill in those sneaky little fence holes.

Remember we dogs don't deliberately try to upset and annoy our humans with bad behaviour, as this leads to disharmony within the pack. When the group feng shui is unbalanced, we are sad and confused. We want to make our humans proud and pleased, because when you're happy, so are we.

Idle paws are the devils work.

The Human Perspective on Behaviour Problems

When it comes to dogs behaving badly there is one thing we always tell our clients and that is, if the 'top alpha dog position' isn't available the dog will never apply for the job. In short, that means if you always show your dog that you are the boss, he will be less likely to challenge you. If you are not prepared to step up to the mark, then your dog is hardwired in such a way that he has to take the lead, it's that simple.

Everyone wants a well-behaved dog but sadly some people never get their wish. The reasons are many and varied but generally it boils down to four key issues:

- The owners selected the wrong breed and temperament in the first place.
- They don't have the time needed to commit to their dog's training and education.
- They are reluctant to be the leader, preferring to concede to their dog's every wish, not realising that from respect comes love.
- They have no idea how to stop any undesirable behaviour.

So regardless of whether you want to be a consistent and fair alpha human or not, the fact is that until you decide to step up to the mark, you won't have the well-behaved dog you crave.

It's human nature to nurture and coddle all living creatures including dogs. We love them to bits and want what we feel is best for them. The problem is, dogs are different creatures that do possess some human-type wants and needs, but are basically predisposed to crave leadership. Without it they can feel insecure, and when they feel insecure they might bark at everything that moves, bite and attack, dig up the garden, chew our possessions, and suffer anxiety, stomach upsets, skin flare-ups and more.

It is hard to fathom that something as simple as 'leadership' can make such a difference to how our dogs behave.

Solving bad behaviour

If you have a badly behaved dog you must firstly make sure that you catch him in the act of the misdemeanour and then correct. Secondly you need to ensure that your timing is precise. It's pointless to allow your dog to run and bark at the back fence then wait till he returns to you before you correct his behaviour. You must always pat your dog each time he approaches (he must never fear approaching you). Never correct your dog after the fact or drag your dog back to the 'scene of the crime'. This is pointless, and your dog will never learn his lesson. He will only learn to dislike you grabbing his collar.

Bark Busters say:

- To solve your dog's behavioural problems, you need to be the top alpha human.

- If you don't step up to the mark as the leader, your dog will.

- Dogs without leadership can suffer from all sorts of behavioural, physical and psychological problems.

- Dogs are hardwired and predisposed to crave leadership.

- You must catch your dog in the act of behaving badly before correcting.

- Never drag your dog back to the 'scene of the crime'; this will only cause complications.

7 The Educated Canine

🐾 Sox's paws for thought

Dogs – play to learn

Humans – learn to play

That this chapter follows on from *Dogs Behaving Badly* is no random act of the cosmos, but a calculated move by me, the four-legged philosopher. At times, I feel there is a cloud of negativity surrounding dogs. Contrary to popular media portrayals, we are not all bad mannered, uncouth philistines, with no appreciation for the finer things in life. *The Educated Canine* is all about training, teaching and tutelage (not behaviour, bribery and brainwashing as Bluey and the CWU may suggest). Education is not a dirty word, nor is obedience old-fashioned. It isn't mindlessly following direction, standing to attention or even wiping our paws, but acquiring skills to take us through the many challenges of life.

Dogs need social competence, an understanding of rules and acceptable behavior and for some lucky canines, perhaps even a smattering of philosophy. Some of us have a natural cunning and intelligence, and take to training like Kelpies to utes. Others are more cerebrally challenged (Poodles, Samoyeds and Rottweilers spring to mind) and need a little extra time to get through the basics. Either way, the result should be the same, a courteous, well-educated canine that is a pleasure to be around and take around.

So where do you go from here? Why not venture out into the big wide world of obedience classes, where you and your dog will benefit from meeting others in a fun, supportive environment.

Unless you live in the back of beyond, chances are there will be a class or club to suit your dog's needs, from puppyhood right through to advanced training for the more intellectual canine:

- puppy pre-school
- basic obedience
- advanced training
- other – agility, tracking, sports, dancing

Puppy pre-school

Puppies are little sponges (albeit furry ones), that eagerly pick up manners and behaviours (good and bad) from their significant others. Staying with mum and our litter mates allows us to develop good doggy social skills, to the detriment of our human interaction. Conversely, if we leave the litter as youngsters (as most do), and stay at home with only our humans as company, we are all in a dither when meeting one of our own species. We need guidance in the formative early months so we can straddle the two worlds without getting a nasty injury. Puppy pre-school is the answer.

You've seen all those glossy advertisements of happy youngsters hanging out with their puppy pals at pre-school? They aren't just PR spin, but the real McCoy. Pre-school is THE place for your energetic, exuberant and inquisitive puppy. They are run by obedience clubs as well as your local vet. I admit to being a bit 'thingy' about the vet (it's that smell and all those nasty associations, you understand) so these classes are a great way to introduce your puppy to the doggy doctor in a positive way. It may even result in some dogs actually enjoying future visits to the vet (is this possible?).

Pre-school offers a pup the chance to romp and play with new chums (canine and human) in a safe, enclosed and supervised area. In all this fun and mayhem, important learning happens too, with basic sit, stay and lead-walking topics explored. Classes usually run for a few weeks, which allow the participants plenty of time to get to know each other. Firm friendships are made and pee mail addresses exchanged. Often the instructors give talks on puppy parenting, behaviour problems and health. A fun time is had by all.

When Snowy was a puppy all those years ago, pre-school hadn't quite taken off as the place to be seen. She skipped this part of her education and went straight to basic obedience. By the time I came along three years later, things had changed and pre-school was quite de rigueur for any pup wanting to make their mark on the world. I recall those early times with great fondness. They would have been some of the best days of my life (apart from that bossy and overbearing Poodle).

Dog obedience – beginners

Dog obedience is primary school for dogs and the next step in our education. These classes are for dogs (with up to date vaccinations, naturally!) from about four months old. Although this is the beginning of our 'formal' training, it is also very much about meeting and greeting other dogs and humans. There is sniffing, leg lifting, tail wagging and patting a plenty. While all this company can equal lots of excitement, it can also mean lots of distraction. It takes a lot of will power to settle to the task and focus: dogs and humans are here to learn. The trainers don't teach us directly, but teach you to teach us, if you follow. This way, we get to practise the lessons in the comfort of our backyards with our human, until the next class. Practice may not make perfect, but it certainly helps to reinforce the lessons.

Snowy's association with obedience classes was short lived:

The whole experience was just so negative. The classes stifled my creativity, the teachers didn't understand my special needs and there was no catering for individual differences. (Snowy 'Free Spirit' Osborne)

Basically, she was a loose goose. After a few difficult sessions, she dropped out, never to return. Her temperament and lack of grey matter meant home schooling was the way to go. In contrast to this drop out, I am happy to report that the local obedience club became my alma barker. I went straight to the top of the class and was an A grade student. There is even the graduation certificate and gleaming trophy to prove it.

Dog obedience – advanced

Here we have the higher learning end of canine obedience, the University of Dogdom. The sky's the limit when it comes to this more advanced training. It all depends on the persistence of the human and the intelligence of the dog. There is the off-lead control, hand signals, jumping and climbing, barking on command, playing dead... impressive, to be sure and great party tricks, but just how necessary, I wonder? Being a pound puppy and a proud graduate of the school of hard yaps, I have never felt the need for further education. I believe my achievements bark for themselves.

Agility

I will agree that some of this agility training is exciting stuff. It just isn't my cup of milk.

I know I COULD jump over burning ropes, crawl through tunnels and balance on see saws, all this in record time in front of a crowd. The question on my muzzle is why WOULD I? The body is strong and supple, but the motivation weak.

Tracking and retrieval

Ah, now here is something I could really stick my nose into. Ideal for those extra sniffy breeds (Bassets, Beagles, Dachshunds, Dalmatians), but suitable for any dog that has the nose, energy and perseverance for a good chase-and-find game. Does backyard bone retrieval count, I wonder?

Competitive sports

There is a range of sports we dogs excel in: fly ball, Frisbee, high jump. All a bit of fun, as long as things don't get too serious. I certainly have excellent mouth/eye co-ordination and with my penchant for soccer, have often wondered if my career could have taken a different direction. Trouble is, these football clubs seem to use dogs as mascots, rather than players. What a waste of talent.

Dancing dogs

I'm sure there are dogs in the world that enjoy boogying to the beat, particularly with the addition of a fetching bow tie or glamorous tiara. It's just that I don't know any. Still, there is no accounting for taste and one shouldn't point the claw; public humiliation may be just the in thing for some.

Residential training

This is where we head off for a bit of live-in training with 'experts' while our humans stay home watching TV. A bit like sending your dog off to Swiss finishing school. I'm not a big supporter of this method. We return, fully trained, to uneducated humans who have no idea what to do with us. Better that both parties are trained together and have a common goal.

If all else fails

There may be some out there who just can't or don't get training. For them, none of these options have been successful. Where to from here? No, the answer isn't back to the shelter or pound and shame on you for thinking such a thought! There is always hope. I am even prepared to stick my handsome muscle-bound neck out and state there is no such thing as an untrainable dog. Just think laterally. Maybe a different approach would work, such as home training, or calling in an expert (sorry, I don't do house calls—too busy with my literary career). Please don't give up— for dog's sake.

Dog training and fun should be synonymous, both for the trainee and trainer. What better way to ensure it is, than to join in the many groups and clubs around the country? These organisations offer support, friendship and expertise for you and the dog in your life.

What we dogs learn in pleasure, we never forget.

The Human Perspective on Education and Training

Good on you Sox, you are one savvy pooch, a dog after my own heart: a dog that knows the benefit of education for canines, and that an educated canine equals a well-adjusted canine.

As the founder of the largest dog training company in the world, it's a foregone conclusion that I would believe in the importance of training your dog, and I make no secret of it. I compare it to the education of children. You would never argue that children don't need their early education or that they should never go to school. So why is there so much debate on whether dogs should be educated and trained?

It's really so simple. If a dog remained within the litter and was allowed to grow up amongst their litter mates, the mother would be responsible for her puppies' education and training. She would set the boundaries, letting the pups know what was expected and what the rules of the pack were. She would be fair and just, not sweating the small stuff, but growling or snapping when the puppies over-stepped the mark. The pups would instinctively know that if they stepped over the line again, they would suffer the consequences.

Once we take on the responsibility of a puppy or dog, we should then take on the responsibility of their education and training; the education and training they would receive if they remained within the litter. About now, you might be asking why? Why should I train my dog, how would it make a difference and why is it so important?

I cannot blame you for asking such a question. It's one I asked myself as a very young child, way back when. As a little girl I rescued stray dogs that had a myriad of behavioural problems. I thought that love could heal their souls and cure their problems.

Well I was wrong. Love was not enough. The dogs also needed guidance and training to stay alive in a human-dominated world full of rules and regulations, a world that could take a dog's life if they were to overstep the mark to bite or attack a human.

A dog that is allowed free rein and is totally overindulged can develop into a creature akin to a spoilt brat that has little or no respect for humans, and that wouldn't think twice about biting or attacking one.

To analyse the importance of training your dog and how training makes a difference to their behavioural problems, let's look at why it works.

Training and to a lesser degree, education, is a subtle, passive way of turning the tables and reversing the pack hierarchy. Unlike the puppy's mum, who can actively assert her authority by snapping and nipping the recalcitrant pups when they do something wrong, you would not fare well if you tried to discipline in that way. You wouldn't want to be nipping your puppy every time he stepped out of line, besides you would get a mouthful of fur.

But there are parallels between a mother dog's training and our training. The mother dog corrects her pups when they step out of line, because there are a set of rules that the puppy cannot break without consequence. The same thing applies to training. You accustom your dog to what is right and wrong and they will quickly toe the line. You can now channel your dog's energies into something positive while you subtly climb the hierarchy ladder and gain a greater communication level with your dog. This gives you the ability to work on their behavioural problems.

So what about those dogs deemed untrainable? Well, I am yet to meet one. It's usually the humans who cause the most problems: those humans who want to gain leadership by just turning up or feel that training and education is cruel or harsh.

Unfortunately the Animal Welfare and RSPCA shelters are full of dogs that belonged to well-meaning people who refused to face reality. I have never met a dog that can't be trained. You just need clear, simple communication, fair and just correction, and consistency to achieve your goal. If you do have a very difficult dog, then call in a professional who can help you calm, train and educate them.

Bark Busters say:

• When humans take on a new puppy or dog, it is their responsibility to educate and train them.

• Dog training is the most effective way to reverse the hierarchy and to stave off behavioural problems.

• There are no untrainable dogs, just owners who don't want to do what's necessary to fulfil their dog's needs.

• If you believe you have a difficult dog, then seek professional help.

8 Bothersome Barking

🐾 Sox's paws for thought

Dogs – our way of communicating
Humans – noisy and annoying

So why DO dogs bark? A vexing question and one with as many answers as blowflies at a bone. We bark because we are bored and lonely, because we are hungry and sad, excited and joyful, suspicious and scared. We bark at other dogs, strange animals, unknown humans and curious objects—we even bark at the moon.

Barking, yapping, woofing, yowling or baying—call it what you will—is simply one of the many ways of canine communication. Of course, the question on every human's lips (and indeed every dog's slobbery muzzle) is when does barking move from normal to nuisance? Problem barking is not just a doggy dilemma, but everyone's business, or at least everyone within earshot. Let us take a scamper down the barking by-ways and look at this issue in more detail.

Guard barking

I can recall my first tentative big dog bark; a stranger was sighted and as a trainee guard puppy, I knew where my duty lay. With a jaunty leap, I was off and woofing. From then, whenever I felt our territory was being threatened—a jingle of keys, a knock on the door, a strange car or an unknown voice—I was onto it, barking like there was no tomorrow. Yes, I was overly enthusiastic, but it was my job, so why did my human get so upset? After a few weeks of confusion and many sprays of water on my nose, I understood the guard bark must be used sparingly. A few short but sharp barks are all that's needed. My human was alerted and my duty fulfilled.

There is no doubt that—without getting too breed-specific or personal—some large black dogs with tan muzzles and feet do take their guarding duties very seriously and are given free rein in the barking stakes. And yes, I will agree that a large number of them are employed for exactly that reason, but some let the power of the bark go to their large vacant heads and give dogs a bad name.

Take Mr X, our local car yard protection pooch. My family and I have been taking our evening constitutional past the northern fence for years, but every time Mr X sees us, he starts the 'All who pass, hear my bark and despair' routine. Quite theatrical, I'll agree, but what a din. Brings a whole new meaning to 'protection racket'—if you'll excuse the rather paw pun. Many times I have tried to explain that two elderly, law-abiding dogs and their humans hardly constitute a threat to his domain, but this falls on deaf, and to be honest, rather unattractive pointed ears.

Bored barking

I am pleased to report boredom barking has never been a problem with me. With an expansive yard, fences which allow me to see through to the world beyond, plenty of opportunity to sniff and whiff on my daily walks and toys to while away the hours, I am a dog replete. Chloe, the Crazy Collie from Clover Close, alas, was not. But I'll let her relate this cautionary tale of woe:

> If ever there was a pup born to herd and destined for greatness it was me: a purebred Collie with champion parents and a faultless heritage. Why, I was rounding up beetles and calculating ewe speeds before I was weaned. Thinking back, I should have been suspicious when I saw

my new owner; not a ute to be seen and not even a whiff of greasy wool.

With my dreams of herding wayward sheep slipping away, I tried to remain positive.

Perhaps they were tree changers and we were headed for a small acreage?

Imagine my dismay when we arrived at my new home, a suburban backyard that would give a guinea pig claustrophobia. Initially, there was a lot of fuss and attention and even a daily walk, but eventually even this stopped.

An active, intelligent working dog, bored and left alone is a dangerous combination. My descent to full-blown barking addiction started innocently with a bit of whining. This progressed to howling sessions and before I knew it, I was a fulltime barker and a dog in serious trouble. It could have ended badly, but luckily my humans took positive action; daily walks reemerged, as did regular agility classes. I had a healthy outlet for my energy, barking was no longer my obsession and Clover Close returned to normal.

(Chloe the Collie)

Aggression barking

The aggressive bark is not something I indulge in often, but is necessary in time of need. A recent encounter with Percy the pig dog—all rippling muscle and studded collar—had me on the back paw, barking and snarling like crazy. I held my ground, but hoped his primeval bark really was worse than his bite. I couldn't decide if he was barking mad or madly barking. Regardless, his human had the foresight to put the beast behind a strong fence, so there was a lot of noise but no action. I gave him a final 'lucky I am on this lead or there'd be trouble' bark and we continued on our way.

Attention barking

The 'look at me' bark is all about attention seeking. Think pound puppies hoping for a home or pampered pooches that feel the world revolves around them. It can also be used effectively to remind those upstairs that dinner is overdue. A variation to this is the 'look at this' bark. Being a dog with considerable life experience, I rarely indulge, however it is common amongst the younger set. First encounters with umbrellas, mowers, phones or any number of unusual things can produce a barrage of anxious barking. If only their humans had spent more time taking them out and about.

Alien animal bark

This bark is usually associated with conniving cats trying to muscle into a dog's territory, but can also be used to chase off marauding magpies, bothersome beetles, tiresome toads and other pesky pests. I have recently been busy keeping the vegetable patch a parrot-free zone, a difficult job in view of the birds' penchant for ripe tomatoes. After a spirited chase I like to finish with a few short woofs of joy, to reinforce just who is boss of the backyard. Being a Terrier, Snowy has the upper paw in the snake sniffing out department. Once discovered, however, we join together in a very distinctive 'snake sighting' chorus. In my experience, this is one warning bark appreciated by humans, regardless of what else is going on in their life at the time.

The Midnight Yapper

This diary extract gives an insight into what turns a mild mannered dog into the infamous Midnight Yapper of Suburbia, known to make grown men (and women) weep.

(Disclaimer: This is a work of fiction. Any resemblance to real dogs or small Terrier crosses is coincidental and a bit embarrassing.)

Another day bereft of walkies. Third time this week. Am a ball of pent-up energy. What happened to a fair day's walk for a fair day's guarding? Can feel the Midnight Yapper questing to be free.

Perfect weather, yet no walk again. With the full moon upon us, am resorting to an after- hours barkfest. Hoping broken sleep will awaken our humans to their responsibilities. Have been resting my throat and body in preparation. And so to sleep, perchance to bark...The Midnight Yapper has returned!

An enchanting evening! The sky was clear, the moon bright and the acoustics perfect. The Midnight Yapper's howls resonated throughout the neighbourhood. Humans looking suitably tired this morning.

No walkies again. Is no walk = return of Midnight Yapper too subtle for them? My kennel mate has some romantic notion that barking beneath a full moon unlocks the primeval wolf lurking within. I have my doubts, but have been enjoying exploring my dark side.

Another walkless day. Checked my BMI (bark to muzzle index). It was high. Waaay too high. Maybe the Midnight Yapper has overdone her nightly vocalisation?

Walkies finally, tired and replete. The Midnight Yapper has been retired—until next time.

(Anonymous)

Frankly, many of the issues surrounding problem barking can be laid (politely) at humans' feet, for they are the experts at confusing messages. One day we are being praised for being vocal guard dogs, the next we are scolded for behaving the same way. All very puzzling. As in all human/dog relationships, clear, consistent rules in the barking department keep everyone, (including the noise-averse family at Number 58) healthy and happy. We dogs are generally easily pleased with simple needs. The return of a favourite human, a romp on the beach, a game of soccer, a juicy bone—all events to be celebrated with a waggly tail and a few judicious woofs of joy. Nothing over the top, mind. With barking, less is definitely more.

He who barks best, barks last.

The Human Perspective on Barking Problems

Barking is one of the most contentious behavioural issues we get asked to solve. We have seen families in crisis, people at their wits' end, neighbourhood disputes, and dog owners prosecuted and fined by their local council, all because of a barking dog. Many dog owners will tell you that dogs should be allowed to bark at will, that it's unnatural to try to stop them and that their complaining neighbours are just trouble makers. Others think a dog should never make a peep and should be seen and not heard, especially the long-suffering neighbours of constantly yapping dogs.

The problem is this: if we as dog owners don't take responsibility in controlling our dogs' nuisance barking, there will be more and more places that dogs will not be allowed to go. There would be far less issues about dogs being allowed in apartments, retirement villages and nursing homes, to name just a few places, if barking could be controlled.

My own dogs never bark unless there is something serious to respond to, and then it's action stations when they do. One time it was a brown snake in the back yard, another time it was someone trying to get into the property, another time it was when one of our dogs had injured itself. If we allowed our dogs to bark all day long, these important situations might have been ignored.

If a dog barks at everything it's like the proverbial car alarm that keeps going off in the wind, or the story of the boy who cried wolf—you'll never know when there is real danger. Also a dog that barks at birds, fire engines, people and dogs passing the property, neighbours, aeroplanes, etc. is going to be doing a lot of barking. This is what we at Bark Busters call 'nuisance barking' and it stems from the dog's feeling of insecurity, which relates back to a lack of leadership and the owner not being the alpha human.

When we are called in, we do not try to stop the dog from barking altogether unless specifically requested. We ensure that the dog's four basic needs are met (food, shelter, leadership, companionship and entertainment) then we work at stopping the nuisance barking. A dog that feels secure in his environment, knowing he has a strong human to look after him, will have no need to do any nuisance barking.

Important point: Barking needs to be cured where it occurs.

Dogs learn by association and therefore any training must be carried out while the barking is happening. For example, if your dog barks at the back fence or at the back door, you must catch him in the act of barking at the back fence or the back door to teach him that you do not approve. Sending him away for training or taking him to a training school will not teach him that he mustn't bark at home. If you have a dog that won't stop barking despite all of your efforts, call in a professional who will come to your home.

There are many things you can do to solve nuisance barking. Firstly start by becoming the alpha human. Be consistent—don't allow something today, then try to stop it tomorrow. Don't open the back door when your dog barks to be let in, instead wait for him to be quiet before you let him in. If your dog runs to the back fence barking or barks at birds etc., correct his behaviour by clapping your hands sharply and correct in a deep tone, praising the instant he stops. By doing this each time your dog barks you will very quickly teach him that nuisance barking isn't tolerated.

Bark Busters say:

- A dog that barks at everything is like the car alarm that keeps going off. It could be ignored when there is real danger.

- If you want to stop your dog barking you must first become the alpha human.

- Stop responding to a dog that barks to be let in. Instead, wait till he's quiet before opening the door.

- To solve nuisance barking clap your hands sharply when your dog is barking and praise him when he stops.

- Because dogs learn by association, all barking must be addressed when and where it occurs.

- If your dog has serious barking problems despite all of your efforts, then call in a professional who will come to the home.

9 Digging is More Than Just Dirty Paws

🐾 Sox's paws for thought

Dogs – gardens are for digging and sleeping
Humans – gardens are for flowers and vegetables

Dogs and digging go paw in paw. To dig is an innate and instinctive behaviour. What could be more natural? It is a noble occupation and one which we dogs share with many other animals around the world. Even humans enjoy a good dirt dig from time to time, although one does have to feel sorry for them with those dreadfully ineffective hands. As to my position on the (w)hole digging issue, I must confess to sitting comfortably in the pro-earthworks camp, even though it is something I 'fell into' late in life.

In view of my natural bias towards doggy digging, I took a quick survey amongst my canine chums to discover what motivates them to interact so passionately with the earth:

It's there. (Benji the Jack Russell)

It's fun. (Sophie the Aussie Terrier)

It stops me from being bored. (Chloe the Collie)

I love the positive synergy that flows from the earth's aura. (Snooks the Greyhound)

It's just like snow, only brown. (Shadow the Husky)

To bury bones and other treats for a rainy day. (Sam the Labrador)

To create a cool snoozing nook in summer. (Sam again)

To create a warm snoozing nook in winter. (And again)

Because I can. (A Doberman and current member of Dirty Dogs Dig Dirt Deep organisation—name withheld on request)

Digging for me had always been a purely practical solution to storing my bones (away from prying eyes). Likewise, my kennel mate was not a committed burrower, but rather a surface scratcher. These were more symbolic digs which did add a certain interest to the boring backyard, but there was no real depth behind (or in) her garden gouging.

I was a mature dog of five when the light bulb moment struck. While attending to a bone hole, I noticed how warm and soft the bare earth was in the winter sunshine. A few judicious digs and presto, we had our prototype snoozing nook. What a serendipitous moment! Being the larger dog, I did the heavy duty excavations, with Snowy finishing off the final trim work. After some minor adjustments and fine tuning, the rewards for our hard labour were a plethora of deceptively intricate snoozing holes to luxuriate in all year round. Fine examples of modern barkitecture.

As any doggy excavator will tell you, a solid dig provides mental as well as physical stimulation. Our nooks are organic and forever evolving, depending on the seasons and our changing needs. We have to consider the trajectory of the sun, potential views, soil type and the optimum hole depth. Snow prefers the 'deep and steep', whereas the 'shallow and wide' accommodates my body type more comfortably. Currently I am investigating the possibility of a bone storage area, for ease of accessibility and to create the ultimate in a multi-functioned nook. Last, but not least, are the tasty by-products exposed during the earthworks: protein-packed lawn grubs, beetles, spiders and the ever popular cicadas.

Of course, it's important to remember that digging isn't all milk and squeak toys. There have been a few regrettable incidents, but as a clever canine once barked, you can't make holes without breaking bones. Naturally, we were distressed when the young master tripped in one of our cleverly disguised snoozing nooks. Who'd have thought a game of soccer could end so spectacularly and that a small human could make such a racket?

Then there was the 'misplaced bone in the vegetable patch' saga. I still wonder what possessed Snowy to hide it in amongst those seedlings. Of course they would grow and disguise the burial site, so there really was no other option but to dig up the whole garden. A dog's bone is sacrosanct, after all. While we couldn't understand the words *per se*, the general demeanor of the humans was one of considerable distress. I told Snowy not to take it to heart. Carrots and beans are overrated and no great loss to the world.

So, to sum up the affirmative side of the dog digging debate— what's not to like? Well, according to many humans— plenty! They take umbrage to the backyard being turned into an archaeological dig, and despair when their dogs refuse to stop. Herein lies one of the major differences between the canine and human species. Humans just don't get doggy digging and employ devious methods to curtail it. Sophie relates her battle of will with her 'no dig' family, which fortunately had a happy ending for both parties:

> There was an escalation of hostilities and a full assault of the back yard from those who want to be obeyed. A multitude of unpleasant things found their way into my excavations—chilli powder, pepper, balloons, water and the ultimate insult—my own poop.
>
> After a long and protracted battle of wills, I was triumphant. The humans embraced my urge to excavate

and provided a dedicated Terrier sandpit. I relinquished the backyard to them and peace returned to Number 10.

Following on the heels of this Terrier tale, I should introduce my big friend (that we shall call 'Houdini' for soon-to-be-obvious reasons) the Staghound from down the street. Houdini is an amiable, easygoing sort of dog, with no great urge to dig and more than happy to while the hours away in his big backyard— as long as he has company. Once his human leaves, this placid pooch becomes an anxiety-riddled escape artist. No ground is too hard, no foundations too deep for this digging dervish. I have given up counting the times he has dug his way out and then spent the day nosing at us through the back fence, avoiding the attentions of the dog catcher.

Houdini usually begins the visit with a few vigorous games of 'fence chasey', which we all enjoy. Having sixty kilos of rippling muscle running up and down your fence is great fun, but only when it is on the other side. When the day comes to an end, his human returns home, until the whole sorry act is repeated the next morning. Houdini doesn't dig for fun or pleasure, but as a means to an end. Here is a dog in desperate need of a fulltime human friend or some home-based canine company.

As you can see, the reasons we dig are as varied as the dogs themselves, which does rather make the human hope for one remedy to doggy digging seem rather foolish. A little bit of old fashioned arbitration might be needed to ensure both you and your pooch are happy with the outcome.

PS: Our snoozing nooks have proved such a hit with the local pack, I'm pleased to report that *Holes of Distinction* is now officially open for business.

Be still, my digging paws.

The Human Perspective on Digging Holes

As Sox says, 'digging' is a natural instinct, and dogs' reasons for doing so are many. They dig to reach insects below the ground, to search for nutrients that are lacking in their diet, to dig a den, to find a cool or warm place to lie, when feeling anxious or just to see what's down there. We receive many calls from dog owners who are at their wits' end because their dog is digging up the yard. They cannot understand why the dog needs to dig and why their scolding isn't working.

Basically the reason that digging is a difficult problem to solve is that most people go about it the wrong way. They discipline their dog after the fact, usually when they arrive home to find the holes that their dog has dug while they were out. The problem is if they can't catch their dog in the act of digging (by now you would have gathered that if you don't catch your dog in the act of the misdemeanour, then he won't catch on) then all of their aggro does nothing but cause a lot of stress for their dog. Remember, dragging your dog back to the 'scene of the crime' does not work.

There's more bad news when it comes to digging and that is, because dogs learn by association you might be lucky enough to catch your dog digging in one particular spot and teach him that this is undesirable, but—and there is a big 'but' unless you're able to catch him digging in every single spot of your garden, then you have little hope of solving the problem. He might catch on that digging in the flower bed is wrong but could just as easily move on to digging under the tree or digging up the lawn.

So how do you solve it?

Remember the four basic needs: food, shelter, leadership/companionship and entertainment. Your dog needs all of these to stay balanced. So check to ensure you are providing these basic needs.

The first golden rule is never scold after the fact. The second is, make sure your dog isn't bored. He needs stimulation, so offer him interactive toys. A company called 'Play and Learn' have a large range of toys that deliver treats and encourage the dog to use his brain. This takes care of two of your dog's four basic needs in one go. Listen to Sox. Provide a digging pit of sand, where you can place his toys. The sand pit is a cool place in summer and a warm place in winter, which is probably the main reason your dog is digging. Last but not least, your dog needs companionship and leadership. We cannot stress this too often.

Bark Busters say:

- Never scold your dog after the fact. Finding a hole and dragging your dog back to it is not conducive to a good dog/owner relationship.

- Provide your dog with interactive toys that deliver a treat. This will fill at least two of his basic needs: food and entertainment.

- Provide a large sand pit. This can sometimes solve your problem quite quickly.

- Remember above all else your dog needs leadership and companionship.

10 Barneys, Bickering and Biting

🐾 Sox's paws for thought

Dogs – happy in a hierarchy

Humans – happy in a democracy

Biting, chewing, nibbling, nipping, gnawing, munching and crunching—so many words to describe such an integral part of being a dog. We are, after all, descended from wolves and the call of the wild is never far below the surface, be it deeper in some dogs (think pampered Poodles) than others.

Don't be fooled by the docile domesticated doggy, all sweetness and light. Behind the face of innocence lurks a slathering beast ready to bare its 48 razor sharp teeth. Mind you, it isn't our pearly whites *per se* that are the problem, but what we sometimes do with them. There is the good (eating din dins, worrying at those infernal fleas, munching on a brisket bone), the not so good (attacking other dogs and animals) and the downright naughty (biting *Homo sapiens*). The biting dilemma is indeed problematic for both canines and humans. Doggy bites are not much fun for biter or bitee and does more than upset the feng shui. It can mean a one-way ticket to the vet, not something any dog wants to experience.

We canines are pack animals and as such, are more than happy in a hierarchical society with humans as top dogs (four legs good, two legs better). Problems surface when this social harmony is upset. Yes, there are the odd occasions when mad megalomaniac mutts try to usurp human leadership (four legs good, two legs bad). In my experience however, the problems are commonly created by humans who deliberately blur the demarcation line.

Egalitarian principles (four legs good, two legs equally as good) in a doggy household leads to confusion and discontent. Who does eat first and just whose bed is it anyway? Then there are the humans who appoint their canines as household leaders (four legs best, two legs just ok). Put a dog in charge and Houston, we have a problem. These 'canine kings' are often small, snappy and self important. What Honey the Chihuahua lacked in size, he made up for in attitude. He ran the human household with an iron paw: sleeping on the beds, eating on tables, sitting on laps. I predicted it would end in human tears and one day it did. Honey broke the doggy oath of allegiance and bit the hand that fed him.

We still don't understand why diddums bit us. We gave him everything. What an ungrateful little dog. After that episode, we decided to put him back outside with the other dogs, but he just couldn't get along with them. In the end, we had to surrender him to the pound. (Mr and Ms Thick – Honey's humans)

Luckily for Honey, he got adopted by an understanding human, who took the time to re-educate him, and this doggy dilemma had a happy ending.

Next we come to fear biting. These poor devils deserve a little sympathy, for their world is full of confusion and anxiety. They bite because they are scared of strange humans, unknown dogs, thunder, water, cars, balls, mowers...the list goes on. I am not a dog that enjoys pointing the claw, however in this case, the blame can undoubtedly be attributed to the humans. Puppies that are fully socialised with humans and dogs, and exposed to many different experiences in their early months grow up to be well-adjusted dogs (that would be *moi*).

Wally the whippet was a sad creature that had spent most of his formative years tucked away in the country, with only his elderly owner as company. A change of circumstances saw him move into suburbia and come muzzle to muzzle with a whole range of unfamiliar and frightening experiences. Once out of his comfort zone, Wally exhibited classic submissive behaviours. Cowering behind his owner, head down and tail placed firmly between his legs, he was a pathetic sight. A sniff too close by an unknown dog and Wally the Wimp morphed into Wally the Wicked, teeth snapping madly. Things could have turned sticky for Wal, but with time and training, he became a well-adjusted and welcoming whippet.

Our duty is to protect and defend our humans, regardless of who or what is the threat. Unfortunately, protective biting (PB) is a grey area and humans often give out mixed messages. Sometimes a protective bite is encouraged and even applauded by humans, at other times you become 'dog non grata'. No wonder the dogs of the world are confused. Let me illustrate this using a completely theoretical situation, in which an intelligent and brave dog (let's call him PP) and his human are enjoying an evening stroll.

In the gloom, PP spies an unknown dog (possibly hostile and closing in fast). He takes his protective pooch position seriously, so is on full alert. PP's owner pulls his lead tighter, making him feel even more wary. Initially, PP tries mediation (back a-w-a-y from my human and no one gets hurt). Suddenly, his human attempts to pat the dog, oblivious to the possible dangers. PP immediately goes into combat mode (must protect human from enemy). What thanks did I...sorry, I mean PP get for this selfless act of defence? Words of praise? A liver treat? Ear caresses? I think not! He is rewarded with a sharp pull on the lead and some very unkind words. As I said at the beginning, the whole protective biting situation is a can of cat food.

On the gentler end of the spectrum are the innocent bites of puppyhood. I recall the rough and tumble world of my litter mates in the puppy pen with fondness. A playful nibble on littlest sister's ear, an inquisitive gnaw at the whelping basket, my first tentative chew of a bone—how else is a pup to learn about the world around them? There comes a time, however, in every pup's life when it's time to grow up. The loss of milk teeth and the emergence of adult choppers marks a dog's coming of age—an exciting time for any youngster hoping to make their mark on the world. A firm maternal paw (or human hand) may be needed at this time to reinforce the fact that uncontrolled biting in polite company is not acceptable. Without this steadying influence, a pup could go on to bigger and most definitely not better things in the biting line.

Where do I stand on the biting issue? As a well-adjusted and socialised individual, I bite only in extreme circumstances: if threatened or attacked by another or if I believe my human to be in danger. I do confess to a particular dislike for Samoyeds, having been barreled over and bitten by an anti-social individual as a puppy. Try as I might, this has been difficult for me to overcome and I do find myself snapping and snarling at the first sight of a fluffy white coat. Luckily, these lightweights are few and far between in my neighbourhood, because this early experience in my formative months has been difficult to overcome.

I will also admit to one incident of owner biting and one I am not proud of. My fascination with cars got the better of me on an afternoon walk and I made a lunge for the tyres, instantly regretting my impulsivity. Battered, bloody and pumped with adrenalin, I was in a state of shock and in no mood to be grabbed from behind, albeit by my own distressed owner. We both learnt from this encounter: I not to chase moving mechanical devices and my human to give me space if, heaven forbid, such a thing ever happens again.

Yes, it is a cliché, but humans often DO bring dog bites on themselves. How many rough and tumble human/dog games have gone sour and ended in blood and tears? Some dogs can understand the fine line between play fighting and the real thing, others have more difficulty. Combine a competitive or dominant dog, a shot of adrenalin and the excitement of the chase and a playful nip can easily become a fully fledged chomp.

Hey, sorry about the finger, Master. Things got a bit serious for a moment. The red mist descended and you know I do like to win. Still, look on the bright side; you've still got nine left. (Faithfully, Rusty)

Sox's 'no no list' of what not to do when playing with your pooch:

- play-slapping (especially around our heads and sensitive muzzles)
- wrestling
- tackle
- tug-of-war
- chasey

Always remember if a game does go wrong, you might end up bruised or bitten, but you'll recover soon enough. Faithful Rusty may end up paying a much more permanent price. So why risk it? Or, as my clever Aunty Boots always liked to bark, 'Better to be safe than sorry.'

Look before you bite.

The Human Perspective on Aggressive Dogs

Aggression from a dog can make the strongest person shiver in their boots. People have been known to leap into the path of a car while trying to get away from an aggressive dog. Dogs show aggression for many reasons: as a controlling tactic, when fearful of something, and when they want to stop a dog or a human from approaching them or in a situation where they feel threatened.

Dogs don't bite for just any reason, unless they have some sort of deep-seated psychological or neurological problems. So let's examine more deeply why a dog will resort to aggression. The aggressive dogs we deal with nearly always fall into two categories: fearful or controlling.

Confused Cujo

Cujo, a two-year-old cross Mastiff/Rottweiler, was rescued from an animal welfare shelter. His owners initially found him to be a docile and gentle dog that showed love for the whole family.

Unfortunately Cujo had no love for anyone outside of the family. He began to bark when visitors arrived and would leap and growl at the windows in an effort to get at them. The owners very responsibly kept him locked up, till the day he broke out and attacked a young boy.

When I met Cujo he was leaping up at the side gate trying to eat me. As we always do, we interviewed the family to see if Cujo's four basic needs were being met. We found he had ample food, shelter and entertainment, but no leadership.

We showed them how to restore leadership by using techniques such as programming and what we call 'threshold control', in which you use your voice to stop the dog crossing a threshold without the 'okay' from the owner. We then left for ten minutes while the owners practised, and told them that when we returned we'd see what had been achieved. Ten minutes later I was knocking on the front door. There was complete silence. I poked my head around the door asking the owners where Cujo was. He was sitting on his bed.

This case history clearly shows that when you reverse the leadership, taking it away from the dog that has no sense of right and wrong, you can quickly stop the aggression. Cujo has never slipped back to his bad ways. He now knows that there is no need for him to carry on every time someone comes to the front door or enters the house. He knows he has strong owners who will let him know when they need his help to repel an unwanted guest.

Tips for dealing with aggression

Identify why your dog is being aggressive. Is it due to fear as in the case of Cujo? Or is it a controlling tactic to stop you or another dog from doing something? Once you know why your dog is being aggressive, you will have a better chance of solving the problem. If the behaviour is fear-based, then it might be simply that you are not acting like the alpha human (there's that term again). If your dog is fearful of other dogs or people, then he feels vulnerable and you need to show some leadership by being consistent with your corrections. Work at gaining control in the home first before venturing out where the problems are more severe.

If you identify that your dog is being aggressive to gain control, then you might need professional help. If your dog is controlling you in an active way, then if you try to reverse roles and get it wrong, you could get severely bitten.

If dog aggression is the problem, reverse the leadership in the home first, following the correction process as detailed in the example above. De-sexing will make a huge difference to your dog's reaction to other dogs. Once you have gained leadership around the home, get a friend who has a dog come to visit your home making sure that the dogs are separated by a secure fence. Then using a water squirter, spray him each time he shows aggression and praise the instant he responds. You will need to do this many times with great results before you progress to more adventurous stuff. It's not necessary for the dogs to fraternise; they only need to tolerate each other.

Bark Busters say:

- Aggression is usually based on two main factors: fear or control.

- Identify why your dog is being aggressive.

- Dog aggression is best controlled through de-sexing, by establishing leadership at home first, and then training behind a secure fence before progressing.

- Dogs display fear aggression if they feel vulnerable. You need to show your dog that you're a strong alpha human.

- If your dog is using aggression as a controlling tactic, then don't risk a serious attack—call a professional.

11 Meeting & Greeting

🐾 Sox's paws for thought

Dogs – greet by licking and sniffing

Humans – greet by handshakes and smiles

We dogs do soooo love social interactions with the *Homo sapiens* species. In fact, sometimes the thrill of a human meet and greet is all too much and we let the excitement of the moment take over. This is often when unwanted behaviours rear their ugly head. And if something isn't done by you, Mr or Ms Alpha Human, this behaviour keeps popping up as often as your canine friend. In the meeting and greeting arena, there are generally two types of dogs, the springers and sniffers. In my experience, neither type is appreciated much by humans.

First to the springers, those excitable and acrobatic individuals that just can't help but make the 'leap of face' when they greet their own humans or meet someone new. For these canines, the higher the better. Why settle for a kneecap lick, when you can go for the head? And yes, I am guilty as charged; although this is one habit I left behind with my adolescence. As a puppy, jumping and licking was my preferred way of greeting my mother. When you are one in a sea of litter mates, it pays to be noticed.

Once I was adopted, I continued this with my humans and I could tell they thought it was sweet. What harm could a four kilogram leaping bundle of pure cuteness do? And then I grew up...and knocked the small human over. Amazing what a difference an extra 20 kilograms can make. There were tears, unkind words and some serious soul searching on my part. Jumping really was for the cats.

Of course, not all dogs 'grow out' of the springing meet and greet, nor are as open to change as I was. Recently, my human was knocked to the ground by Crusty, the neighbour's exuberant dog. Coffee, muffins, glasses and bits of human went everywhere. All very nasty. (Like any good and faithful hound, I rushed to her aid and offered my vacuuming services; the floor was cleaned in an instance.) What was Crusty thinking? He had spent the previous day with us, and yet he behaved as if he hadn't seen her for months. I gave him a good sound barking to on the pitfalls of springing, particularly because of his size. I'm not suggesting he has a weight problem, but his resemblance to a Weddell Seal is uncanny. Imagine if it had been my human's elderly father, or young nephews? Crusty was nonplussed by my reprimand:

> *That Sox thinks he's so smart, just because he's writing a book. Well I've been a jumping sort of dog since puppyhood and I'm not going to change just because HE told me to. There haven't been any complaints from my significant humans and until there is, I'm sticking with it...and I'd better not end up in that book, or there'll be trouble.*

Now to the sniffers of the world. Meeting and greeting human visitors is one of life's pleasures and at my abode, the welcome routine follows a time-honoured tradition.

- My acute hearing picks up a knock on the door or an unknown human voice.
- I give a few short, sharp guard barks to alert my humans.
- Once the human welcome is complete, it's my turn to meet and greet.

Being a dog of the old school, I am a firm believer in the introduction ritual and always extend the courtesy of a 'sniff and whiff' to any new acquaintance, be it canine or human. Humans may be pathetic smellers, but they make fascinating smellees. Here the vertically challenged canines amongst us are at a disadvantage, being restricted to an ankle and calf sniff or if they are lucky, perhaps a furtive whiff of knee cap. Human body parts to be sure, but rather insipid. Taller dogs (lucky me) are in a direct line to more interesting areas. As any dog worth their weight will tell you, a quick smell check and all is revealed: family, friend or foe. Sometimes I may follow this up with a quick lick, just for confirmation, you understand.

Unfortunately, humans do not 'do' sniffing. Nor do they understand it and in my experience, they certainly don't appreciate it. Unfortunately, it is here, amongst the soft curves of human physiology, that the chasm between dogs and people is most evident. A penchant for human sniffing is viewed rather dimly:

He is the perfect dog in every way—except for that embarrassing habit of sniffing people...and not just their hands! It isn't so bad with friends and family, we can make a joke out of it, but not with new people. The worst are the women. He has his nose up the dress and sniffing. I just want the floor to swallow me up. Do you ignore it or say something? (Mr & Ms Embarrassed – PP's humans)

A little exploration into dog anatomy at this stage may help to explain this behaviour, for we canines were born to sniff. Large olfactory cortex? Check. Long muzzles? Check. Moist and mobile nostrils bursting with millions of glorious scent receptors? Check. The ability to detect the subtle and minute odours of the world around, thousands of times better than a human? Check. Regardless of whether we are a sniffer dog or simply the dog next door, we are the smelling super stars.

So what is it about our sniffs and whiffs that causes so much angst amongst our humans? Fear of exposure? (No scented secret is safe and y-e-s we can smell if there is another dog in your life.) Or perhaps it simply comes down to the 'cold nose' situation? There are even rumours that suggest some humans are embarrassed by their dog's sniffing—perish the thought!

Although I am at a loss to understand the reasons, I am dog enough to admit there is an issue here that needs resolving.

Following is my plan to smooth the way to happier canine/ human interactions. And proving once again that I am a dog of substance that is prepared to put theory into practice, this has been trialled at our abode with positive results. I now embrace a more sociable and 'down to earth' approach to greeting, which keeps my paws firmly on the ground. Please note the use of 'Snowy' in this example is purely representative and has no bearing on any real canine.

Sox's Simple Solutions

- Stand still and strong when Snowy springs – remember you are the alpha human.

- Keep your arms and hands in front.

- Follow up with a disapproving growl (practice in the shower for a convincing act).

- Reward appropriately (pats, treats, squeak toys) when Snowy is back on the ground.

- Congratulations, you have now made a friend for life. Dogs don't have a quota on human friends—we believe very much in the 'more the merrier' principle.

- Remember, no kneeing in the chest or standing on paws— that's just mean.

Sox's Simple Solutions (especially for puppies)

- Get down to puppy level by bending or kneeling (great view here and isn't that floor interesting?). This would end the need for jumping and help to reassure the nervous puppies among us. You humans are so tall and can look rather scary.

• Allow us to come to you for a hand sniff. Oh go on—hands aren't as sensitive to cold noses and surely you can't find that part of your anatomy embarrassing? It IS supposed to be a compromise, after all.

• Give us time to run you through our smell check.

I still get cravings for body 'sniffs and whiffs', but with the support of my significant humans, I am working through this.

There are no strangers here; only friends you haven't sniffed.

The Human Perspective on Dog Manners

The majority of 'jumping up' problems actually stem from the way humans react to dogs. It's the things people do when they meet a dog that make a dog behave in a silly way. Jumping up is one of the by-products of this. People have no idea the problems they cause for dogs, the details of which could take up a whole other book.

Many people when they meet a puppy for the first time will go overboard with so many *oohs* and *ahhs*, excited chatter and body language. This immediately sends the puppy into a wriggling, writhing mess, a puppy that thinks they should respond by leaping about excitedly the instant they see a human approaching.

Also, most people will allow a little puppy to jump up on them because it saves them bending. This cements the idea in the dog's mind that if they see a human, they have to behave excitedly, jump and leap about and then leap up and lick their face. Owners of puppies should bend down, rather than allow the puppy to jump up for his pat.

There is also an issue with the way people deal with 'jumping up': they try to jump backwards to avoid the pain and destruction of their clothes, and in an attempt to avoid the dog's advances they push it down with their hands. What they are actually doing, in the dog's eyes, is emulating the way another dog instigates 'play'.

How to solve 'jumping up'

It's really very easy to cure 'jumping up': you just have to adopt the correct body language. All you have to do is emulate what dogs do when they want to stop another dog from jumping on them. They freeze their actions, they show their dislike for the other dog's actions through their lack of body movements and

95

the other dog gets the message very quickly. In rare cases where a dog keeps going and fails to heed the body language of another, the offended dog will ramp up the messages to the offending dog by growling and snapping. Most dogs will heed these reprimands and will move away quickly.

Now all you have to do is follow the dog's lead by freezing your actions the instant the dog leaps up, keep your hands still and locked in front of you while you growl in a deep voice. Then clap your hands sharply. Now because we don't want our dogs to go away, we must also add a little to what the dog does. That is we need to make sure that our timing is 'spot on' and once our dog's feet are both back on the ground, we must praise immediately, preparing for the dog's quick return where he will again try to jump up. So in essence, it's 'bad dog' and clap when the dog's feet are off the ground, praise as soon as his feet are on the ground, and repeat again and again till he gets the message and he will, if you get your timing right.

Bark Busters say:

• Our over-the-top antics are largely to blame for the way dogs behave when they greet us.

• If you want to stop your dog jumping up, then you must adopt the same body language as that of the dog: don't back away. Freeze your actions, stand your ground and keep your hands locked in front.

• Ensure your timing is 'spot on' by correcting the moment your dog's feet leave the ground and praising the instant that his feet hit the ground.

• Owners should bend down to pat their puppies rather than allowing the puppy to jump up for his pat.

12 Walking Worries

🐾 Sox's paws for thought

Dogs – any weather walkers
Humans – fair-weather walkers

A daily outing is an essential for all dogs, regardless of size, breed or age. The sofa loafers might be happy with a stroll to the shop, while the Terrier types love an energetic work-out. It's not so much the size of the walk, but what you do with it: the quality, rather than the length.

A sniff to catch up on the outside news, the all important tree wee, maybe a scamper in an off-leash area— all stirring stuff which we dogs adore. Of course, walks aren't all about us. Humans benefit too. An excited pooch at your door is about the best motivator for a lazy human to get up, get out and get active. A perfect win/win situation for both species. All we need is the sunrise and the fading music…if only it were that simple.

Prior to writing this chapter, I asked Snowy to do some market research to ascertain exactly what the current issues facing the dog walking public were. The response to her survey was overwhelming, with a staggering two humans replying. The main dog walking worries were:

- pulling on the lead
- aggression towards other dogs
- not returning to the call
- chasing vehicles

One hundred per cent of respondents stated their current dog needed further training in walking on the lead. These were groundbreaking results and called for further investigation. Snowy set about digging up the dirt and once the dust settled, the culprit was outed, proving that even creative geniuses have their flaws. And so we move on to the chapter topic—walking worries—starring the four-legged philosopher himself.

A walk offers up so many endless chasing possibilities—cats running provocatively across the road, the rustling of small creatures in the undergrowth, a motorbike zooming past—that some type of canine constraint is *de rigueur.* Sox's personal tried and true selections are:

Collars

- Buckle - the normal collar for those that have overcome canine yearnings to chase
- Halti or head collar – the gentle, yet firm collar for dogs that are still wrestling with their pursuing demons
- Body harnesses replace collars, good for dogs with neck and throat problems

Leads

- Retractable lead allows the free spirits to roam but still keep the wildlife safe from marauding mutts

I give the paws down to check chains—called choke chains by dogs for good reasons.

When introducing dogs to any new harnesses or collars, don't forget to keep it short (the experience that is, not the lead) and follow up with food rewards.

New equipment + food = pleasant experience

(That Mr Pavlov had nothing on the four-legged philosopher.)

Pulling on the lead

Don't know about you, but as a sensitive canine, I am sick to the back molars with the 'Who's walking who?' put down. Yes, lead pulling is one of the main reasons humans stop walking their dogs, but there is no excuse for negativity. It is simply that our love of walkies can often work against us.

To be in the great outdoors with our alpha human is just about every dog's idea of nirvana. The world is our oyster, but there is so much to do and so little time: roads to travel, other dogs to sniff, footpaths to conquer, trees to baptise. Ambling along at snail's pace just doesn't work for some feisty types. They want to smell the roses AND the chip packet. Time is a wasting and some humans don't have the same sense of urgency, so we pull and pull and pull and…end up back home. No, the truncated walk is not a happy event, resulting in a cranky human (with sore arm) and an unfulfilled dog (with full bladder).

Sox's Simple Solutions

- Practise heeling at home before venturing into the exciting world beyond the backyard.
- Whenever your dog pulls on the lead, stop, make him sit then start again. Reward with treat.
- Burn up some energy at home before venturing out. We always start the afternoon activities with a robust game of ball chasing. This knocks the edge off our excitement and our energy.
- Halti collars work well for controlling extra boisterous dogs, particularly handsome black Cattle Dog types.

Aggressive walkers

Yes, me again, the model walker, until I see another dog. Then mild-mannered Sox turns into a slathering beast. I can blame this on a frightening experience in my formative years. My humans, Snowy and I were enjoying our afternoon walk, when, without warning, we were under attack. I had always believed Snookums, a large and unfriendly mongrel, to be an 'all bark no bite' sort of dog (well you would with a name like that wouldn't you?). Turns out he was, but only when behind a fence. In all the chaos, I managed to hold my ground and slip in a nice upper bite to the left ear. From that day on, I adopted the 'get in first' philosophy. Where was Snowy in the mêlée? Behind me, in principle, but actually being held aloft, well away from harm. Being a small, lightweight dog does have benefits at times.

Sox's Simple Solutions

• Socialise, socialise, socialise. The more varied experiences puppies and young dogs have, the better they are able to cope.

• Avoid walking past large dogs of unknown temperament when they are free and wild (especially ones with silly names that you may have inadvertently passed comment on).

Nervous walkers (starring Snowy for a change)

If your dog seems nervous, apprehensive or very under-confident when out on a walk, it could be linked to a negative or frightening event that happened in the past. (That Snookums has got a lot to answer for, and I won't apologise. It is a sooky name.)

Sox's Simple Solutions

• Socialise, socialise, socialise. As with fear aggression, it is the early months that play an important part in a dog's view of the world. Keep them away from any potentially frightening experiences (and dogs with issues about their sooky names).

• Keep your dog at a weight that can easily be picked up in signs of trouble.

NB: To any small dogs that have let themselves go, when the big dogs roam, you're on your own tubby.

Not returning to the call

Yes, I...we are guilty, but there were mitigating circumstances (aren't there always?). There was this fox you see. First one we had ever seen. A REAL fox, and Snowy has REAL Foxie blood coursing through her veins. This was what she was bred for, her moment in history, and her destiny. In two shakes of her Terrier tail, she was gone, locked in to the chase. What was a dog to do? My pack member was off in the distance, barking excitedly and urging me to join her. In one wiggle of my tail stub, I too was off, ignoring my humans' cries. Of course it ended in disappointment. It had to really; a couple of aged pet dogs chasing a wild fox. What were we thinking? There were recriminations aplenty, too. Snowy blamed me, I blamed her and our humans blamed us. I do think 'the untrainable chasing the inedible' jibe was a little unkind.

Sox's Simple Solutions

- Lead us not into temptation – avoid fox habitats if you have a Fox Terrier.
- Ditto for other 'chasing' breeds.
- Reinforce the 'come' command with a food reward and lots of attention.
- Don't overuse the come command – only call us back if you really mean it.

Chasing vehicles

Yes, guilty once again and I can't point the paw at Snowy this time. The four-wheel drive had been passing us each afternoon for months. So why did I, in one reckless moment of madness, try and round it up? I did manage to bite the front tyre for a millisecond, but it was such a short moment of triumph. Apart from a few scratches and bruises, the worst injury was the teeth loss. Since that day, I have found myself gazing longingly at cyclists, motorbikes, even joggers, so am aware my addiction is in remission, not cured.

Sox's Simple Solutions

- Don't allow car-chasing canines access to their addiction. Keep them on the lead near traffic.
- Get jogging or cycling friends to stop and squirt recidivist dogs with a water pistol.

And so ends this sad and sorry chapter. Some readers may be surprised or even disappointed to hear my admission of guilt. Others may be secretly pleased, proving that the tall puppy syndrome is alive and well. For me, this has been a humbling, yet cathartic experience. It has made me realise that I, like any dog, have my faults and failings. I also believe hard work, liver treats and lots of tummy pats in the sun can overcome many of life's challenges.

You can teach an old dog new tricks.

The Human Perspective on Going Walkies

There's no denying it, for many of our four-legged friends 'going walkies' is the highlight of their day. Most dogs will leap and dance about the moment their lead appears, heading for the door, dragging their owners behind them.

As Sox says, there are very few people who could honestly say that their dog walks perfectly on the lead, regardless of how hard they try. There is a very good reason for this. Dogs are natural 'pullers'—they instinctively pull on a lead as soon as they feel any pressure on it. This is why people are able to easily teach dogs to pull sleds.

Why people have 'dog walking' problems

Some dogs view walking as an exciting adventure—they're eager to get going and to sniff out new smells and meet old friends—while others view a walk as a venture into enemy territory, a place where other dogs have established their hierarchy, and will bark their claim to that territory as the interloper goes by. Is it any wonder that some dogs become 'dog aggressive' on the walk? They are constantly challenged as they try to run the gauntlet, hoping they can escape with their life intact.

I personally do not take any of my dogs street walking as there are too many people who have little or no control of their dogs, nor do I take them to parks where dogs are allowed 'free range'. I much prefer to pop them into my car and find a quiet place devoid of dogs. The dog walking utopia—no stress, just play time.

However, there are people who, whether through love or necessity, take to the streets for their daily walks. Here are some tips on how to keep you and your dog safer while walking. Take some treats with you, and at the first sight of a dog running free or approaching you and your dog, drop a treat in the dog's path and keep walking. Cross the street (safely) and keep walking. Do not attempt to stop, even if the dog approaches your dog, just keep walking and keep your dog walking, the idea being that if you keep walking you will be distancing you and your dog from that dog's territory quickly. The dropping of the food is designed to change the marauding dog's focus, away from you and your dog and onto the food. Keep dropping the food as you go, walking out of the area as quickly as possible.

Teaching your dog not to pull on the lead

When teaching your dog to walk properly on the lead, you need to firstly have the right tools: a good-quality lead and the right collar. When we go about teaching a dog to walk on a lead correctly, we do as Sox suggests. We first work at increasing the owner's skills, encouraging them to practise in their backyard and hone their skills, getting them to stop the forward progress each time the dog pulls on the lead. However we don't use a fixed collar, we use a Bark Busters 'communication collar' that is similar to a fixed collar but has the ability to communicate a message to the dog. And should not be mistaken for a chocker chain collar.

Our Bark Busters training collar is made of leather or cotton, with a small chain section that the lead clips to, and closes up only to the size of the dog's neck; it cannot tighten beyond that or choke the dog. Neither can it slip off the dog's neck, unlike a fixed collar. Yet it sits loosely on the dog's neck till the dog pulls to the end of the lead, then each time it reaches the end it will hear the 'click' sound.

We do not use fixed collars for walking, although we promote them for every dog to hold their ID. A fixed collar is not a training device. All a fixed collar can do is lift body weight or put pressure on the dog's neck. By walking a dog with a fixed collar, you'll only encourage him to pull on the lead: he has no alternative, as the collar communicates nothing to the dog. Yes, you can pull your dog back using the lead and collar but the dog will just pull straight out to the end of the lead again. We recommend a pure cotton lead; it's soft on the hands as well as being strong and reliable.

Bark Busters say:

- Some dogs view 'street walking' as a walk into enemy territory. For safety's sake, you might want to exercise your dogs in an area devoid of other dogs.

- Street walking your dog has its risks, but if you are adamant about walking your dog down the street, then take treats with you and if approached, cross the street (safely) and keep walking, dropping the treats as you go.

- Dogs are pullers—they will naturally pull when a lead is pulled taught.

- Practise walking your dog correctly in your yard first before venturing out, stopping the forward progress each time your dog pulls on the lead.

- Fixed collars are not a training device but are invaluable for holding the dog's ID.

- We believe that the best walking collar is one that communicates something to the dog when it pulls, and one that sits loose on the dog's neck when it stops pulling. This is the quickest and most effective way to train a dog to walk properly on a lead.

- When possible take your dog for a walk on the quiet side—a place devoid of other dogs.

13 The Birds and the Bees

🐾 Sox's paws for thought
Dogs – de-sexing rules
Humans – de-sexing is cruel

I want to be upfront and completely candid about where I stand in relation to sex and the single dog: it gets the paws down. Before I am accused of being a prudish goody four paws (gee that Sox is such a prudish goody four paws), my belief has nothing to do with morals and all to do with the problem of unwanted dogs.

All dogs should be de-sexed, unless their humans are registered breeders. A contentious point of view and no doubt it will put a few cats amongst the Terriers, but it is something I feel very strongly about. So, if you are hoping for some in-depth information on breeding bluebloods, this is not the place and I am not the dog. Stud dogs? Pregnancy? Whelping? Nope, sorry, completely foreign world to this big black dog. Remember, I might be a celebrity canine, but I am also a de-sexed male mongrel.

So, if there are way too many puppies, where do they all come from? Let's take an average mongrel bitch and call her Jane Dog. Jane hasn't been de-sexed, either because her humans haven't bothered or perhaps she's a stray. Puberty hits and she goes in search of the love of her life. The relationship fails and soon she finds herself a single mum to a bunch of cute, wriggling little pups. Now that she has started the breeding cycle, she can lick her independence goodbye, because from now on, Jane and her offspring will be kept very, very busy.

In six years they will produce...wait for it...67,000 puppies. Consider also that the majority of those cute little bundles of joy will end up in animal shelters, waiting desperately to be adopted. Sadly, most won't be.

So, apart from stopping unwanted pregnancies, are there any other benefits to de-sexing? You bet there are and as an RSPCA pound puppy that was given the chop at a very early age, I bark from a position of authority.

- First up, we de-sexed dogs are healthier, calmer and I daresay a lot happier without being plagued by amorous thoughts.

- Life is a lot less stressful and frenetic. Some individuals wear themselves to a frazzle, trying to be the neighbourhood stud. All that hanky panky can't be good for a dog.

- We are less likely to stray or be involved in fights.

- Bitches have a reduced risk of tumours, uterine infections and ovarian cancers.

- Males reduce their risk of prostate cancers.

- We get a great tattoo to brag about. In the right company, this can increase our street cred significantly.

- Puts a stop to all that urine marking some dogs seem obsessed with. I enjoy a bit of scent marking as much as the next dog, but I always restrict it to the great outdoors. Indoor marking is so vulgar.

- Dogs are less inclined to display antisocial, aggressive or territorial behaviour.

At this point, please allow me to digress a moment and move onto the 'mounting mutt', an issue many humans find very embarrassing. The urge to mount usually hits dogs in their reckless teenage months. A surge in hormones and the sight of the good-looking bitch down the street can get a dog hot under the collar. In older dogs, mounting can sometimes be a dominance display.

De-sexing often stops this behaviour and there have been many a dog whipped off to be 'tutored' after an attempted affair with a visitor's leg. A change isn't guaranteed though. Getting the chop did nothing to curb Benji's proclivities. Although his passionate liaison with the lounge chair was doomed to fail, he still continues his 'humping hound' routine with inappropriate partners: tables, cushions, other dogs, slow-moving cats. What he needs are a few well aimed water pistol shots to help him rethink his 'positions'.

All fine and dandy, but are there any negatives to de-sexing, I hear you ask? There is a definite feeling amongst some in the canine (and human) world that de-sexing somehow makes us less of a dog. I have had similar comments expressed in relation to my natural bob tail. We do live in a tail-obsessed society, but length does not define you as a dog and bigger does not necessarily mean better. My missing 'T's' have never caused me any embarrassment. I'm as good as the next dog, regardless of what they may possess. Nor have I ever been worried by any tail or testicle envy. As for making a canine undogly, well I think my 30 kilograms of buff body and superior intellect makes a mockery out of that idea.

The other canine complaint is that of weight gain and yes, there is some truth in this. With no members of the opposite sex to impress, some dogs do run to flab and this is where you can help. Dogs only get fat if humans allow them to, so do Fido a favour and cut down on his food. Of course, just because a dog has had the snip, doesn't mean he is destined to a life of indolence and gluttony. Snowy is a case in point:

Spayed bitches get fat! If I had a bone for every time I heard that, I'd be a retired bone baroness by now. I had the op way back in '95 and haven't put an ounce of weight on. It's just a matter of self control and not letting yourself go.

So, when is the best time for de-sexing? While many animal shelters do the deed on male dogs at an early age (six to eight weeks, like yours truly) most vets recommend the best time for female and male dogs is about six months old (exactly the age my kennel mate had her op). This brings me to my next point. Some kind but misguided humans believe a bitch should have one litter of puppies before she is spayed. This is a load of cats' swill and is not supported by those in the know or the four-legged philosopher. All it does is bring more unwanted puppies into the world. Rather than take my word for it, I asked Snow if she felt she had been 'cheated' by her early spaying. This was her response:

My procedure gave me the opportunity to focus on what I wanted from life. As it turned out, my skills lay in management, and over the years I have climbed the pack ladder. I'm a career bitch to the bone and way past the 'mother dog' routine. There are no maternal urges lying dormant in this little Terrier cross. Whining puppies, puddles on the floor, discipline—makes my nose go dry at the thought.

What can I tell you about the operation? Well not much really. It happened so far back in my past that the memories are vague and fleeting. I do know we boys get it easier than the bitches, as our operation is less invasive (pays to have everything out in the open sometimes, eh fellows!). In the interests of good journalism, I attended the weekly gathering of the Cut Canine Club (CCC) a fairly small group in our territory, unfortunately. They were all keen to reminisce about their de-sexing experiences to their guest visitor:

Didn't like missing out on my din dins, but the big cut was a non event.

One moment you are checking out the juicy tabby on the table, the next you are counting the purple spotted bones dancing on the ceiling.

I didn't react well to the anaesthetic and was sick as a dog. Took me a couple of days to recover, but then I was back into life with a renewed vigour.

It was such a relief. No more sneaking out for forbidden trysts. Parenthood? Haven't missed it at all.

Being an original pound puppy, I've seen the result of uncontrolled dog breeding, and it isn't a pretty sight. I was one of the lucky ones. Being selected as a life companion for the Osborne household certainly meant I fell on my paws, but I still remember the palpable sadness of the puppy pens. So many dogs and so few humans looking for a pet. Do your dog a favour and get them de-sexed. It's a no brainer.

Neutered young, best in the long run.

The Human Perspective on De-Sexing

Sox and I are in complete agreement here: a de-sexed dog is a happier, healthier dog, and the benefits are enormous. As Sox says, there are some who feel that de-sexing is totally unacceptable. Some people will cringe at the thought of de-sexing a male dog, yet have no qualms about the de-sexing of females.

As the ex-manager of an RSPCA shelter, I have seen first-hand the effects of the 'over production' of puppies. There are so many puppies that are taken straight to animal welfare shelters as soon as they're weaned simply because no one wants them. De-sexing would alleviate that problem almost immediately.

There are far more puppies being bred than there are people who want them, and while these poor unfortunate puppies and dogs sit in animal welfare shelters looking for homes, there are thousand more being born into a world that cannot accommodate them all.

The argument that if you de-sex a dog you make them less of a dog could not be further from the truth. I personally have two Rottweilers—one male and one female—both rescued from people who were struggling to cope with them. I have had both of them de-sexed. Diesel my male dog, is very much admired by everyone, including those macho men who cringe at owning a de-sexed male dog. I use Diesel to drive home the fact that de-sexing does not make a dog less of a dog, and it's the smartest thing you could do. Diesel is as 'macho' a dog as you can get and he's warm and friendly to all dogs and people, yet protective when he needs to be.

Bullseye the Casanova

Many years ago I was asked to find and train a dog for the stage play Oliver! I found an entire male (not de-sexed) Bull Terrier at the local pound and called him Bullseye (the pounds were not routinely de-sexing their dogs in those days). Bullseye's training was successful and he performed beautifully on stage, receiving many great reviews and accolades from the local media.

A short time after the stage play ended, my husband and I had to go overseas leaving Bullseye with my daughter. A short while later she rang us with some bad news. Bullseye was desperately trying to escape and our daughter was finding it increasingly difficult to keep him in. Also he was beginning to fight with her male Labrador and she now had to separate them. Without any hesitation, we instructed her to have him de-sexed as soon as possible, as we believed that would fix the problem. The procedure was an overnight success, and Bullseye settled down to wait patiently for us to return.

If you are not convinced as to why you should de-sex your dog, then talk to the staff at an animal shelter—they'll tell you how important routine de-sexing is.

Bark Busters say:

- De-sexing does not make a dog less of a dog. It makes them healthy and happy.

- De-sexing reduces the dog's urges to fight other dogs and escape.

- There are far too many puppies being born for the number of homes available.

- De-sexing would reduce the number of unwanted puppies and dogs sitting in animal welfare shelters.

- Visit an animal welfare shelter and talk to the staff and see the dogs waiting to be re-homed.

14 The Dirty Dog

Regular grooming isn't just about keeping your dog clean and tidy. Grooming time is when you, the alpha human, can reassert your dominance and strengthen the social bond between your pack members. All that washing, cleaning, clipping, brushing and stroking mimics the mutual licking and grooming behaviour of our ancestors. Just think of the fancy brush as a replacement for a dog tongue and the conditioning shampoo simply an up-market version of dog slobber.

Beaut brushing

There is a dog coat type to suit every human's taste: long, short, curly and fluffy and every combination in between. Before you choose that cute little ball of fluff, think to the future, to a time when the dog of your dreams spends a glorious day in the country, splashing gaily in muddy creeks, running excitedly through the undergrowth and rolling in the week-old dead possum. Long hair = lots of work.

If you are lazy (my human) or busy (my other human) or busily lazy (my human's offspring), you would be better with a short-haired dog. We are low maintenance, 'wash and wear' and quick drying. Round of applause, thank you.

First up, buy a dedicated dog brush, because we don't want your old cast off. Who knows where it's been? Regular brushing is important as it removes dust, grass and plant debris, loose hair and dead skin (a polite term for doggy dandruff). Even short-haired dogs need regular brushing. Why not multitask and do a tick and flea check at the same time?

The fine art of dog brushing is not difficult to master or mistress (political correctness, thy name is Sox). Brush against the grain initially to get deep down, and then go with the coat. Watch for tangles and burrs in the long hairs (didn't I warn you?), or you'll have your dog howling. Don't forget to go to the end of our tippy tail and all the way down our legs. These pooch parts are often forgotten in the grooming rush. I do enjoy a spot of grooming, but with my hectic schedule, we sometimes only have time for a quick brooming. This is a more relaxed rustic affair with the straw broom.

Bathing bother

The cleaning *cause célèbre*—dirty dog versus clean canine—evokes great passions on both sides. Why do humans wash dogs? Are dogs an overwashed species? What is wrong with a good stench up? Being an irregular bather and proud of it, I don't think much of the zealous 'clean 'em every week' types. A lack of washing hasn't held me back. Being of English descent, my humans are supportive of my stand on this issue. Unfortunately, this isn't always the case:

> *A dog can't be too smelly or too dirty. (Wallis the Dalmatian – The Duchess of Dirt)*

> *Dogs weren't meant to be greasy. (Ms Clean – her human)*

Some dogs hate baths so much, the very thought of one creates extreme behaviour:

> *Will devote some time tonight rolling in mud and excrement. In these unsettled times, a dog's best defence is a good stench up. (Stinker the Samoyed)*

Others don't mind the washing *per se*, but find the whole bath ritual distressing:

> *I have suffered the ignominy of a public washing and grooming. This was an unprecedented break with protocol. As befits my position within the pack, I have previously been accorded private bathing. (From Midget Bones' Diary – Memoirs of a Mongrel)*

If the duck poo perfume gets too overpowering and you really must wash your companion, use a proper dog shampoo. Unless your pooch is modelling at Crufts, forget the heavy duty stuff. Most of us don't want extra body, defined curls or revitilised locks. What we do want is warm water, followed by a good towel dry. Our foredogs may have been happy frolicking in icy mountain streams, but your average Fido on the street isn't. When the whole sordid affair is over, don't be surprised if your dog gets an attack of the post-wash crazies. All the shaking, running around and rolling in the grass is part of the ritual. Our bodies are now blank canvasses, ready for re-anointing at the first opportunity.

My kennel mate is very much the self-clean dog. Many are amazed by her quick makeover from dirty dog back to snowy dog. Apparently it's all about using the other dog's bedding to wipe off the excess mud??? Must follow this up...

Skin situations

Skin problems drive dogs mad, forever scratching and biting at the itch that never dies. The cause of your dog's infernal itching could be many things:

- fleas
- mites
- food or grass allergies
- bacterial or fungal infections

Sometimes it can even be brought on by stress:

Poor old Buster had a skin disorder to be proud of. It's his nerves. Been like that since last winter. If any dog had reason to complain about their lot in life, it's Buster. His humans ran a service station out west and he divided his time between dozing in the sun and urinating on tourists' tyres. Lived the good life until the 'other dog' came along. Small, yappy, fluffy and annoying: it's a familiar story. Once she moved in, Buster was out.

The only consolation is that skin problems are easy to spot. You don't have to be too in-tune with your dog to realise something is wrong. Humans sometimes decide to medicate their dog and purchase over-the-counter unguents and lotions. This just won't do as these can dry out our skin and hair even more. You start out with a dog with a bit of an itch and before you know it you have a full-blown hair loss. Not a good look for any dog. Best to trot along to the vet and get a professional opinion.

Coat couture

For long- or curly-coated dogs, the full body clip is best left to the professional cutter. Just make sure she (they invariably are) doesn't follow the trim with some fashion bloopers (I'm thinking bows, glitter and ribbons.) Just keep repeating 'dog, not Christmas tree', until she gets the picture. Home trims are acceptable only when your dog is at the 'hair blind' stage. Oh, and also if the coat is so long and thick that you, other canines and even Fido himself aren't 100% sure which end is which. Then it's a case of kindness. No one wants to be seen trying to feed the wrong end of a fluff ball.

Teeth tidying

Dental disease is all about halitosis, tartar build up, gum problems and teeth loss. It's the last point that has me worried. How can we be canines without our canines, if you see my point? Snowy and I have spent most of our lives as oral hygiene novices. Apart from being bone enthusiasts, we didn't even know such a thing existed (dog toothbrushes, what an idea!) until the fateful day Snow went for a check-up. Twenty-four hours later she returned with a bad case of anaesthetic droop, five less pearly yellows and a story of woe that took hours to retell. Our humans suddenly became oral hygiene born-agains. The place was awash with chicken flavoured paste and dog toothbrushes. Snowy would have none of it. She'd got to 12 without any of this dental care nonsense and that's how it was staying. She may be small, but she's determined. Lesson to be learnt—start brushing your dog's teeth from an early age (and in private please, think of our street cred).

Ear edifying

Oh I suppose I should mention this, although neither I, nor my kennel mate suffers from ear problems. DIY cleaners can be purchased from the vet, but get some professional advice on how to do the deed. Deaf dogs are not big in the pet popularity stakes. Some dogs, particularly those with long dangly, droopy-whoopy excuses for ears, can get infections. Not enough air flow I suspect. Best idea to check for infections is to get up close and personal and give his flappers a good sniff. Any ear odour and it's off to the vet.

Claw clipping

Daily constitutionals keep our claws in check. All that grinding and wearing away on the bitumen. Not all dogs get this opportunity and do need their nails clipped regularly. This can be problematic, because many dogs also hate having their feet and nails touched. No early training again, eh? Best try the age-old dog sweetener: the food reward. There aren't many dogs that would continue to fuss, when there's a liver treat to focus on. Nails, what nails? (I'm starting to slobber just thinking about it.)

Body image is so important these days that even dogs have to put up with a lot of externally imposed ideals. The proverbial 'dirty dog' is fast disappearing beneath mountains of specially formulated canine cleaning products. And while most of us don't really mind a bit of grooming fuss and attention, we simply ask that before you start reaching for the dog soap, remember that cleanliness is not necessarily next to dogliness.

A dog by any other name would smell as sweet.

The Human Perspective on Dog Hygiene

When it comes to grooming, some dogs resist their human's efforts to the very end. The owners lose patience and send their dogs off to the grooming parlour where they are more accustomed to dealing with difficult dogs. This is not to say that your dog will be better behaved, it's just that the groomer might be far more determined to reach their goal than you are.

Grooming should definitely be started at an early age and always carried out on-lead. Remember that your puppy has no idea what you are trying to do, and will at first look at it as play. The lead gives you control, allowing you to correct any unwanted behaviour and preventing your dog from trying to escape the process.

Bark Busters say:

For easier grooming, practise the following process:

- Place puppy/dog on lead and start with a couple of strokes of the coat with a brush or comb, praising as soon as he accepts the brushing with little or no resistance.
- Gradually build on the process till he accepts the brush movements.
- If you find it far too difficult to gain control, try giving treats, but they must only be given when your puppy stops struggling.

To accustom puppies/dogs to bathing:

- Tie your puppy or dog's lead to a secure post and start with a very small trickle of water on the feet only.
- Keep going till he relaxes, then reward with praise or a treat.
- Build on this till he stops struggling.

To accustom puppies/dogs to hydro baths:

- Start by placing your dog in the bath without any water present.
- Offer a treat each time he enters, and give lots of praise.
- Then add small amount of water, praise and lots of encouragement.
- Build on this until your dog allows you to top up the bath without reaction.

Remember: Your puppy/dog has no idea what you are doing: this is alien to him. You need to be patient while he learns what you want from him.

Skin irritations

Skin irritations are many and varied and as Sox has mentioned, can be caused by stress. We regularly encounter dogs suffering from skin irritations coupled with upset tummies, caused by the responsibility of running a complete household in which there is no resident alpha human. This is more common in situations where a very timid dog that would never in its wildest dreams become pack leader, had no choice but to step up and apply for the job because its owner was not willing to be the alpha human. These problems were cured almost overnight when we showed the human how to take the pressure off their little dog and become the alpha human.

Princess Forlorn

When we first laid eyes on a little Shih Tzu named Princess she was a sorry sight to behold. Her owners had called us in to solve her barking, but what we found was far worse. She was sleep deprived from guarding the family all night. She also had a chronic skin disorder, dry coat and tummy upsets. She was one very stressed dog. We also discovered that she had no bed to sleep in, was left to roam the house at night and spent her whole day and night barking at every sound she heard.

We spoke about the four essential needs of a dog and saw that Princess was lacking two of those needs: leadership and shelter. We also advised her humans to change her diet from a low-quality food that contained harmful colourings and preservatives to a raw or a high-quality prepared food devoid of colourings and harmful preservatives.

Once Princess's owners altered their behaviour and became her alpha human, she made a full recovery, her coat soon returned to its natural lustre, and she now gets a good night sleep. There are many other reasons for skin irritations, some allergy related, some diet related, so seek professional advice from your vet to identify what is causing your dog's skin problem.

Dental hygiene

I can honestly say I have never had to use a toothbrush on any of my dogs' teeth over the past 30 years but I know dogs that need to have their teeth brushed. The only difference between their dogs and mine is their diet. My dogs always eat raw food and the 'toothbrush dogs' eat prepared food. So if you feed prepared packaged food, then you may need to regularly brush your dog's teeth. There are some pleasantly flavoured doggy toothpastes on the market that your dog will love. If you feed your dogs a raw diet, the chances are that the raw meaty bones will clean their teeth while they eat.

15 The Healthy Hound

🐾 Sox's paws for thought

Dogs – wet nose good
Humans – wet nose bad

Take a good look at the dog on the front of the Canine Cuisine can and then look at your dog. Now back to the Canine Cuisine dog. How does Fido compare? Same bright eyes, bushy tail and gleaming coat?

Let's hope so, because we dogs really do live blameless lives. No smoking, alcohol, recreational drugs and very few Big Mac burgers means we should be in the pink (white, brown, black or brindle) of health. All we ask from our humans are regular vet checks, some preventative care and a pro-active approach.

Don't mention the 'v' word

No matter how healthy your puppy or dog is, there comes a day when they will have to go to the V-E-T. No need to say the word out loud, we don't want to create panic. On the subject of vets, chose them carefully. Look for someone who is understanding, patient and knowledgeable (golden fur and big brown eyes are an added bonus, but fairly rare). I like to build a rapport with my vet early on. After all, this is a human who will be having a close relationship with my bottom for many years to come. My very first visit to the vet was a confronting experience, a coming-of-age, and every dog has their own story to tell:

> *Vet day and I will admit to an initial reluctance to embark on the journey. I refuse, however, to make any apologies*

for the urine, the scrabbling paws or the snarl. What red-blooded dog would go blithely, knowing the fate that awaited them? (Ms 'S' the dog)

The waiting room was bad enough. The scent of desperate dogs pervaded the place and I had to suffer the ignominy of sharing floor space with an incontinent cat. Unfortunately, it got worse when I entered the inner sanctum. Even now, I find that the written word falls short when describing the horror of that thermometer wielding vet...how does a dog look the world in the eye after suffering such humiliation? (Mr 'S' the other dog)

So that your dogs/puppies don't develop vet aversion—like our two completely anonymous contributors—make the visits as positive as possible. Special treats go down well with most canines. The way to our hearts really is through our stomachs. The first visit should involve a full check up: eyes, ears, mouth and all other orifices (the least mentioned about that the better) and any vaccinations due.

The other 'v' word

Vaccinations are one of life's unpleasant necessities, but far better than the infectious alternatives: canine hepatitis, parvovirus and distemper to name just a few. Very nasty and to be avoided at all costs. Puppies should start their vaccinations when they are between six to eight weeks old, and these should continue regularly throughout their lives. Snowy always gives a little yelp when she gets the jab (such a drama queen), but thick-skinned Sox barely notices.

Don't rely on your dog's memory for the annual vaccination (we're dogs, not elephants). You can update the calendar, planner or iPhone, but most vets send out reminders. Our vet practice even sends the letters to the dog of the house. I do so enjoy having an important piece of mail addressed personally to me.

Infernal internals

No use beating about the intestinal gut, the worm foursome (tape, round, hook and whip) are nasty little blighters, but nothing for a healthy dog, with worm medication coursing through their body, to be afraid of. There's a certain amount of stigma attached to getting these parasites, and at the first mention of the 'w' word, there is a mad chorus of denial from the humans. 'My dog doesn't get worms' (that's what you think). Parasites aren't snobs and are happy to worm their way into any dog's insides.

Did I say dog? My mistake. Some worms also enjoy a good human intestine to settle into. So if you have been putting off buying the worm tablets, do it, if not for your dog, at least for your insides. Yes, I know giving the tablets to your dog every three months is a pain, but it could be worse. You could be the one who has to eat the stuff.

On the worm administering subject, humans generally try one of the following approaches:

- Disguised in a treat – this is never going to work. All dogs know you should beware of humans bearing gifts.
- Ground up in milk – hello, remember our incredible noses?
- The humiliating and doomed 'shove tablet down the throat' manoeuvre.
- Luckily, most humans eventually discover the chewable wormer. A tasty treat and good for us to boot. A win/win situation.

Of all the low-down parasites, heartworm is probably the nastiest. Heartworm is spread by mosquitoes biting the unsuspecting dog and injecting infected larvae into layers of skin. Sounds unpleasant and it is. The good news is it is easily prevented using daily or monthly tablets, or a yearly injection.

External parasites

Fleas are so yesterday, so help your pooch be the 'no fleas on him' type. With the vast array of treatments available—powders, sprays, rinses, collars, spot on applications—there is no excuse for having a flea bag in the family. We tried a few different treatments, but have recently gone over to the spot-on applications. Neither Snowy nor I enjoy the process, but the end (being flea and tick free) justifies the means (having unpleasant liquid anointing our bodies). My ears are attuned to the opening click of the pipette long before my human emerges with her vial of nastiness, disposable gloves and guilty smile. We can't complain though, as she always sweetens the deal with a liver treat.

Ticks are thick and strong in our neck of the woods. They blend in with a dog's hair which makes the little blighters hard to see. Even with regular sprays or rinses, there's no substitute for a good old fashioned tick check. We canines get to lounge around while the alpha humans in our life caress and fondle our bodies. What a great bonding session. And best of all, this should occur EVERY single day that ticks are active. Although I haven't been worried by ticks, Snowy has had a couple of close calls. Give her a ring if you have a few days spare to hear the story.

Pudgy pooches

Any chapter on healthy hounds would be incomplete without examining the weighty issue of pudgy pooches. These dogs don't just take up too much room on the couch; they have an increased risk of diabetes, arthritis, joint and heart problems.

While some breeds are naturally slim (Whippets, Greyhounds), others do have a genetic tendency to a more generous figure. In this, the long haired dogs of the world have an advantage. All that fluff can disguise a multitude of second helpings. We short coats have no secrets. An extra kilogram and it's out there for the entire world to see. I agree my ribs are harder to find than they used to be. It is also true the doggy door has been enlarged a number of times, but as everyone knows, muscle is bulkier than flab. And yes, I am eating a weight management dog food, but only because I like the taste. And thank you, I am aware the name 'Fatty' is being bandied around behind my back.

Anyway, if I do have a weight problem—and I'm not admitting anything—I know exactly what to do about it. Cut down my food and increase my exercise. Not exactly rocket science, Snowy. (If I hear about her wasp waist once more! Wasp natured, more like.)

Warning signs your doggy is not well

Keep a close eye on your dog and if he doesn't look well, he probably isn't. Most dogs aren't malingerers, although the poor pathetic pooch routine does come naturally to a certain breed which also starts with 'p'. Be pro-active, but not panicky, concerned but not neurotic. Granted, it may just be an overindulgence of bones, but it could also be something more serious. Keep a close eye on your friend and if things get worse, give the vet a call if you notice these symptoms:

- loss of appetite
- lethargy or extra sleepiness
- discharge from eyes or ears
- coughing or vomiting
- hair loss (ignore for Mexican Hairless pooches)
- at the risk of being indelicate, don't forget problems in the nether regions

Your dog's long term health and well being rests with you. It is a big responsibility, involving money, time and dedication, but one which you will be amply repaid in love, licks and never- ending tail wags.

A healthy hound is a happy hound.

The Human Perspective on Health and Wellbeing

The most important factors to ensure good canine health are a safe, protected, stress-free environment and a strong alpha leader who provides for their dog's needs: these include good veterinary care and a natural, balanced diet.

Don't mention the 'v' word

It is vitally important to your dog's health and wellbeing that you find a local vet who has a nice 'kennel side manner', who offers treats (as Sox recommends) and who makes you and your dog feel comfortable.

Unless your dog has had an unusually traumatic experience, there's no reason why he should fear your veterinarian. They are animal-loving people who have devoted many years of their life to learning just what makes animals tick and how to keep them healthy and happy. The vet can supply preparations to prevent against worms, flea and ticks; as well as administer yearly immunisations to ensure that your dog remains free from infectious disease.

If your dog hates going to the vet, one method to help him overcome his phobia is to take him along simply for a treat. Most vets or vet nurses will be more than happy to help you with this exercise. If you do this several times, then when it comes time to go for a check-up or yearly vaccination, you'll find that your dog will pull you though the door, looking for his treat.

Another method is to first take your dog to a place that they love, then the vet, then the place they love again on the way home. It creates a pleasant association in the dog's mind, thus making the vet experience a much happier one.

Watching your dog's weight

There is no reason why your dog shouldn't be fit and trim. You are in full control of everything that goes into his tummy. It's not like he can go to the fridge and grab an ice cream, or demand lollies and chips while at the supermarket. To my way of thinking, one of the easiest things in life is keeping your dog healthy and slim because you are the one who controls his diet and exercise regime.

Dogs don't have the stresses of life that humans have, such as financial worries, relationship anxieties or the pressures of business and work. So you would have to wonder how dogs become overweight. It sometimes boils down to the fact that many people treat their dogs as little humans on four legs. They feed them human food and totally over-indulge them to point of obesity and sickness: they are, in fact, loving their dogs to death.

Keeping your dog slim has its challenges, because you're used to seeing them all the time and those kilograms can sneak up without you noticing. One sure way to keep a watch on your dog's weight is to use the 'eye check' method. You simply view your dog by standing above him. Focus first on the shoulders then run your eye along your dog's body, down to its hindquarters. Your dog's body should be basically a straight line, from shoulders to hips on both sides, neither going out nor in dramatically. If your dog's tummy is protruding, then decrease their food intake. If it goes in, then increase the intake. You can easily keep an eye on your dog's weight this way.

Another way is to measure your dog's tummy at its circumference and tie a knot where the circumference ends. Then use this piece of string to measure your dog's tummy regularly and if you find that the string is not reaching fully around from start to knot, decrease your dog's food. Likewise, where the string begins to overlap, you know your dog is losing weight and you then decide whether you need to increase or maintain his intake.

One sure fire way to keep your dog slim is to ensure that you don't feed any processed sugary foods. Also, keep in mind the amount of food you fit on your own plate and then compare your portion size to that of your dog's and reduce his amount accordingly.

Bark Busters say:

- You have the power to keep your dog healthy and fit.

- Avoid feeding your dog highly processed food such as breads, cakes or sweets.

- To keep your dog healthy, find a local vet who makes you and your dog feel comfortable.

- An easy way to keep track of your dog's weight is to use your eye, lining up the body line from shoulders to hindquarters, making sure your dog's shape does not go out or in dramatically.

- Measure your dog's tummy with a piece of string to monitor his weight gain or loss.

- Finally, remember that your dog's stomach is nowhere near the size of yours, so adjust his portions accordingly.

16 Balls, Bones and Other Fancies

🐾 Sox's paws for thought

Dogs – old bones are delightful
Humans – old bones are disgusting

All dogs have their favourite recreational pursuits which help to pass the day and stave off boredom: chasing the ball, a quiet bone chew in the afternoon sun, sucking on a beloved blanket or even digging up the ultimate rock. Each one innocent and blameless—to a point.

The question on every thinking dog's muzzle is when does a hobby, folly or quirky foible become an obsession? Is there a dark side to all this fun? There is no easy answer, but being a clever canine, I'll have a shot at it. I believe the fine line is crossed when a canine's passion begins to interfere with everyday life. Let's have a look at four common doggy delights and see what sordid secrets may be buried there.

Balls

Well, what decent dog doesn't enjoy a good ball game? Not many I would suggest. Chasing, catching and chewing the ball prey appeals to the wolfish predator lurking within the mild-mannered domestic dog. You might think it is an innocent bit of fetch in suburbia. To a highly trained killing machine like me, it's a primal struggle of life and death (without the messy bits). A robust game of ball is also a healthy, fun way to bond with your pooch. Remember, you're alpha dog, do get in there and lead the chase.

Afternoons at our place wouldn't be the same without the soccer game. Lots of kicking, chasing and running around. Sometimes I even catch the ball on the full—in my mouth, no less. That always elicits a round of applause. Our backyard is large and steep, so it doesn't take long before I'm panting like a cart horse.

Snowy runs around ineffectually, mainly exercising her vocal cords. Apparently, it's because I 'take over' and won't let her play (might is right, Snowy). She likes to reminisce about her pre-Sox heyday, when balls would tremble at the sight of her terrible teeth (ho hum). There was even a 'death corner', where her overzealousness was the cause of many a punctured ball.

We both admit to relishing ball playing, but can enjoy it in moderation. Balls enhance, not dominate our lives, unlike a certain little Aussie Terrier of our acquaintance. When Sophie heard I was writing a section on balls, she was keen to contribute. They are definitely her passion:

> *Hello there readers. Sox has asked me to tell you about balls. Balls? Did someone mention balls? Where? Must chase ...sorry, where was I? That's right, telling you about my hobby, which is balls. Any size, colour, texture. I don't care about the details, just the balls. Love 'em. Hang on, is that a ball? Got to go...*

So ball play, whether an innocuous pastime or a hard-core habit, really isn't a problem, unless you count 'ball boredom' syndrome, an affliction suffered by many humans, including, Sophie's. Yes, we can be demanding of our humans at times and I agree having a slobber-covered ball constantly dropped into your lap, or nudged against your leg can be repetitive. But what alternatives are there? Balls are inanimate, so we really need your throwing power. And as this is really the only 'issue' with balls, it seems a small indulgence on our part. For those humans who like to mock our ball fancy, let me mention one word 'golf'. Repetitive and boring...hmmm. I think I'll leave it there.

Bones

When the sun is bright, the sky blue and the scent of rotten
bone drifts languidly in the air, all's right with the world.
(Old Philosophical Pooch saying)

And so onto that most delectable of fancies—the bone. Bone connoisseurs can be neatly divided into two camps: the 'meet 'n eat' types that prefer their bones fresh and cheeky (my kennel mate), or the 'paw 'n store' dogs that enjoy a twice buried, cellared bone (the four- legged philosopher). My very favourite is the brisket bone, aged to perfection in the clay soil. The problem with burying bones for the future is forgetting the location, a position I found myself in recently. Snowy suggested a bone diviner, but I don't believe in them. There was an old Beagle at the pound that claimed to have the 'scent' and could locate a bone just by waving his muzzle about. Only thing he turned up where a couple of ancient boots and a rusty dog food can. No, I called in the professionals. Bone Busters are expensive, but they're worth it. By mid-afternoon I was surrounded by my redolent stash.

Yes, dogs take the whole issue of bonership very seriously, thank you very much. Unfortunately, there are those in the canine world that take this too far. These dogs show no restraint. No matter how many bones their kind-hearted and handsome kennel mate offers them, they are never satisfied and want more. This is the ugly world of bone obsession which can have ramifications for backyard harmony. While this type of bone-driven behaviour can occur in any dog, it is more common in certain breeds (Terrier, Terrier-cross). I have looked upon the face of bone obsession and it is not a pretty sight.

It will be no surprise when I divulge that Bone Bitch—you met her in Canine Communication—is a Terrier cross (and often a cross Terrier). She provides an insight into the sad world of the Boneoholic:

I like to think of myself as Ms Average: settled, reliable, predictable. I'm all of these things... until I get a fresh bone and turn into a savage, slathering Bone Bitch. There is no room for friends or kennel mates—only my bone. I guard it for hours on end and even get stressed when flies try to land near my preciousssss.

If there are concerns that bone obsession is lurking within your dog (or kennel mate), challenge them to take the test:

- Do you become irrational and aggressive if others approach your bone? (yes, she does)
- Are you obsessive about the safety of your bone? (absolutely)
- Do you really need the bones for medicinal reasons? (no, she doesn't)
- Are you chewing bones alone? (yes, she might be hidden behind the car, but I can still hear her)

I don't want to be the one that points the obsessive bone, but it the collar fits, Ms Bone Bitch, then wear it.

Sucking

Snowy holds the theory that all dogs have a secret fancy, it's just a matter of digging deep enough. As she is keen to lead the exposé, I want to come clean and admit to a penchant for sucking. Nothing over the top. I could stop any time I want. Just a funny little foible, done in the privacy of my own bed. Really, it is no one's business but my own. Besides, nothing has been harmed by it. Well, yes, there was the unfortunate time I overdid the sucking on the cushion. And I had forgotten the time I mistook my human's shirt for my beloved blankey (they looked so alike). But it all came out in the wash (the slobber I mean), so no long-term damage was done. Glad I cleared that up. Everything is out in the open, so over to you Snowy.

I know this is Sox's book, but feel it's my duty to tell the readers that he isn't Mr Perfect Pooch. He has an obsession with 'sucky blankey' that's unhealthy in a dog of his years and goes way beyond a 'funny little foible'. It all began a couple of years ago, as my diary records:

> Sox has taken up what I call 'pig snouting'. Chews the blanket with the very front of his teeth which pushes and flattens his nose. Looks just like a fat, black pig. His bedding is soaked with slobber and the noise is driving me crazy. Clickety, chew, clickety, chew...it never ends. He reckons he has a deep psco, pysoh, psycho...something 'cos of being a pound puppy. Yeah, well, how come it's taken ten years to surface?
>
> He's had a go at my coat, Saturday's washing, my human's pants—nothing's safe from his sucking mouth. Anyway, gotta go. I can see a magpie after my bone...

Rock chewing

Finally, a habit neither Snowy nor I indulge in, but one that is surprisingly common amongst the doggy fraternity. Our friend Kimba was the original rock hound with a hard-core habit. Once she'd chosen the rock victim, it was hers, no matter how deeply buried in the earth. She would then parade it around, firmly grasped between her jaws, and wait for the gasps of admiration and astonishment. As her habit grew, so did the size of the rocks and her neck muscles. It wasn't long before the rock addiction began to impact on her life. First up she lost most of her teeth, then her job. Real guard dogs don't have teeth stumps. From then, things spiralled out of control and she wound up at the pound. Just lucky that kindly human came along. And who'd have predicted he owned a quarry. Now there was a mutt match made in heaven! Heed this cautionary tail and discourage your dog from taking that first experimental chew.

Although this chapter has certainly been a revealing 'warts and all' one, it's important to be open and honest. No dog wants their hobby to take over their life, with all the associated problems: relationship breakdowns, unemployment, bone breath, worn teeth. Remember the old adage—everything in moderation (except sucking).

A ball (bone, blanket or boulder) of beauty is a joy forever.

The Human Perspective on Obsessions

It's true, as Sox says, some dogs just love balls. Dogs enjoy the thrill of the chase (this is a natural instinct) and they are attracted to movement, including fast-moving objects. Balls provide our dogs with much-needed exercise and 'entertainment', one of their four basic needs. As Sox has pointed out, dogs need the human element to make balls more interesting and interactive, yet they still love balls, sometimes to the point of addiction.

One main reason that dogs like Sophie the little Aussie Terrier have become addicted to tennis balls is that they react to the dog's bite. The action emulates the reflexes of prey. Sounds a bit scary, I know, but dogs love that experience: they depress the ball biting down with their strong jaws and the ball bounces right back at them. This creates endorphins in the dog's brain that can lead to ball addiction. The other reason dogs love balls is that they get to interact with their human and if they use their head in the right way, they can actually gain leadership position. How do they do that? They do that by instigating the play. They will grab the ball each time their human appears, dropping it at their feet or lap or nudging their human with the ball till their humans throw it.

The way to prevent your dog taking control and therefore undermining your attempts to attain top alpha position is to ensure that you and you alone instigate the ball game. So keep the ball with you and take it out when you want to play. If your dog runs off with the ball, end the game and walk away. Most dogs will catch onto this and bring the ball back, especially if they want the game to continue.

Bones

Bones are a great way for your dogs to get the much-needed calcium into their diet, but they must only be fed in their raw form. Bones are best if they are meaty and soft, such as ribs, wings and flaps, avoiding necks and oversized bones.

Dogs bury excess food such as bones and meat to preserve it and to save for consumption later. The warmth of the soil acts to cure the bone, preserving it without changing the molecular structure. The process of cooking, however, changes the molecular structure, causing the bones to splinter when the dogs chew them, sometimes creating intestinal damage and occasionally death.

A bone can bring out the worst in some dogs. They can become very protective of THEIR bone, growling when other dogs or humans approach. If that becomes an issue, it isn't necessary to discontinue bones altogether; just feed small, soft bones such as raw chicken wings, which your dog can consume quickly. This will alleviate the problem of guarding bones.

Bark Busters say:

- Dogs love tennis balls because they react and reflex to their bite.

- To prevent your dog from undermining your alpha human status, make sure you, not your dog, controls the ball game.

- Raw soft bones are the only bones you should feed as cooked bones can be dangerous.

- If your dog has bone-guarding issues, feed smaller bones such as raw chicken wings that can be consumed quickly.

17 The Four-Legged Philosopher and Other Animals

🐾 Sox's paws for thought

Dogs – fauna is a threat to our territory
Humans – fauna is welcome in the garden

Recently I was taking a well-earned break from book 'channeling' duties. Gazing over my backyard dogmain, the solitude was broken by the dulcet tones of Snowy yapping at the neighbour's cat. Suddenly I had a *Dog Logic* epiphany. So much of the book was focused on dog/human relationships. What about dogs and other animals?

Had I been a little remiss, perhaps even arrogant, ignoring the other creatures of the world? This chapter will go some way to redressing this imbalance. While I know little about the interactions of Holly, the country Collie (sheep, sheep and more sheep?), I can confidently relate my own suburban backyard experiences (cats, rats, bats and assorted other riff raff). Snowy and I rule this territory with iron paws and defend it vigorously from interlopers:

> *We shall fight them on the lawn, we shall fight them in the vegetable patch, we shall fight them in the skies, and we shall never surrender. (Old Philosophical Pooch saying)*

Cat

Proving I am a dog unafraid of the big issues, first up is the contentious canine/ cat conflict. Our tenuous relationship with the feline species goes back a long, long way, through years of hostilities, tension and misunderstanding. At issue has been competing territory (human laps, beds and the backyard) and just who is the companion animal of choice. I am dog enough to concede we may have lost some ground in the territorial dispute. Dogs put in a big effort at guarding and protecting humans, yet we are often shamelessly left out in the cold, while lazy cats have the run of the house. This succinctly highlights our philosophical differences—dogs work hard for humans, cats work hard for themselves. But it isn't all bad news. Further investigation reveals just how discerning the Australian public is: there are a joyous 3.7 million pet dogs and only 2.2 million cats (2.2 million too many, but that's a personal view). Yes, 'C' precedes 'D' in the dictionary, but the anagram for dog beats 'tac' paws down.

While Snowy and I are pleased we live in a feline-free household, the accusation that we are 'catists' is uncalled for. Why, there are a number of cats living in close proximity that we don't chase. (No, Snowy, no need to mention the fence between us and them.) Anyway, some of our best friends are…well…there was…um… Gus, our dearly departed cat next door. He was a large tabby with loads of attitude. When Snowy was an impressionable puppy, Gus got in early and landed a vicious upper claw to her nose. An uneasy truce settled between them. Although things changed when I arrived on the scene, Gus kept out of our way, unlike his annoying replacement, Shadow. This cat parades provocatively next to our fence, making suggestions that we 'get together' to discover our feline side. In your dreams, you mad moggy. I have seen the result of feline fraternising in Curly from Number 18 and it is a demoralising sight.

Curly spent his formative weeks as the only puppy in a cramped cage full of mewing kittens, desperately trying to fly the canine colours in a sea of feline urine. In the end it got too much for him. There's a definite taint of cat, which no manure rolling will cover. That bizarre high pitched bark and unhealthy grooming sends shivers down my spine. There is a strong element of catophobia amongst the neighbourhood pack and this sort of behaviour doesn't do him any favours, especially with the catnip rumours. Snowy swears she saw the foul-smelling substance in his kennel, but I'm prepared to give the poor bugger the benefit of the doubt. Any dog that cleans his face with his paws deserves a bit of sympathy.

Rats and mice

My early dealings with these little fellows were positive. How could you dislike creatures that thoughtfully nibbled through the dog food packet? Why, there was enough spilt kibble for Snow, me and the rat's extended family. But Snowy, being a Terrier, would have none of it. Called me undogly and explained that humans and rodents don't mix. Keen to do my bit in the war against the rodent peril, I joined up. An extract from Snowy's memoir reveals the ferocity of our battles that year:

Fresh rat manure alert. My highly sensitive Terrier nostrils are twitching with anticipation.

I have fulfilled my destiny; the sighting, the pursuit, the snapping jaws, the satisfying crunch of rat bones.

This ratting business is not all plain sailing. Last night received flesh wound to the muzzle. Gus offered his 'rodent reduction' services. Says as we're neighbours, he'll do a 'two for one' offer with his cat crew. I encouraged Sox to see him off the property.

My nights are taken up with rodent patrol and I'm losing valuable beauty sleep.

Card in my kennel promoting new business called 'Rat Busters'. Suspect Gus is behind it. Have buried in back yard, after soaking with copious amount of urine.

New recruit for night duty. Private Sox is doing a satisfactory job at Rodent Patrol. Can finally rest.

Private Sox woke me several times to advise of enemy movements. Convinced him to debrief in the morning.

Morning report by Private Sox. Three dead. Two were squashed when he sat down. Am nominating them posthumously for the 'Unluckiest Rodents of the Year Award'. The third casualty had no mark on it. Private Sox mentioned he had been retelling his life history to stay awake, so suspect poor devil died of boredom.

No rodent stench infects our premises. We are victorious.

Every now and then, some hardy rodents attempt a re-settlement in our garage, but it never gets beyond the initial reconnaissance. These are the times I am pleased to have a 'catch and dispatch' Terrier as a kennel mate. She really is something to see.

Birds and bats

Snowy and I spend a lot of time involved in bird skirmishes, although unlike the rodent situation, our humans are fond of these feathered irritants. Magpies are the worst, with their arrogant strutting, preening and dropping of dirty bombs. These pesky pilferers are happy to make a 'grab and fly' attempt on any leftovers. They are a canny enemy and restrict their visits to the afternoon when our humans are around. We can do nothing but whine with frustration at the injustice of the situation. There is some sense of satisfaction, however, if we have chicken for dinner. These meals fit perfectly into the long term plans of ridding the world of our feathered foes. Only once have we tasted the sweet tail feathers of victory. The stupid pigeon hit the window in full flight and was dead before it dropped, like manna from heaven, right next to Snowy. Even now, years later, she still yaps about it with awe.

Bats are common in summer evenings when the mangoes are ripening. Between you, me and the pee post, they are welcome to the stuff, but I know our humans feel differently. Snowy and I do our best at defence, but it's hard to get too worked up. Now that we are older dogs, the lure of our beds is stronger than the call of the wild. We put on an impressive woof and bark show until the lights go out upstairs. This is our cue to retreat inside, our guarding reputations intact.

Toads

Toads really are dirty creatures, with dirty habits. Snowy and I go to great lengths planning which leftovers we'll keep for breakfast, when along come the toads . They help themselves to our food and rub their disgusting toad odour on whatever is left. Their poisonous reputation is fearsome, but I am far too clever to attempt open warfare. Rather, I give my distinctive 'toad in the dinner bowl' bark, which brings my human down in an instant. Then we have the satisfaction of seeing our arch enemies take flight—all the way down to the bottom of the yard.

Snakes

Another creature unwelcome in the backyard, by humans and dogs, although I'm not too bothered. Not in my heritage, much too Snowy's disgust. She keeps a tally of kills on the side of her kennel. Trouble is, as she gets older and slower the snakes are fighting back. The last few years she has taken a number of bites and ended up at the vet—sore, sorry, but unrepentant.

As for the lizards, frogs and other smaller creatures which share the yard, we feel they are no threat to our territory or our bone stash. To this end, we can adopt the very Zen 'live and let live' principle. Or at least I can. Snowy's is more 'live and take chase', but then once a Terrier, always a Terrier.

You can't make a silk purse from a cat's rear.

The Human Perspective on Other Animals in the Household

Dogs are very social, and if introduced to other animals early in their development or with specialist training, they can learn to tolerate any other animal in the household. It is important that animals coexist happily if harmony is to reign supreme. At least a ceasefire can exist between the animals, and this is achievable through the efforts of a strong alpha human.

The alternative is complete anarchy, and we have seen many situations where the whole household was in 'lock down' due to conflict between the dog and other animals living on the same property. The other animals ranged from cats, pet snakes, rats, mice and chickens, to large stock animals such as horses and cows. In helping humans gain a peaceful treaty between all of their animals, we would always commence by showing the owner how to be their dog's alpha human and demonstrating how all introductions should be carried out.

Cats

Think about it, cats generally don't run up and attack dogs—they will usually keep their distance or try to run away. It's only when the dog runs at the cat or if the cat is cornered, that the cat will strike out to repel the attack. So the general rule is: control the dog and the cat won't bother the dog, and a brokered truce can be achieved. In some cases, cats and dogs (once the dog stops running at the cat) can live in harmony and even become good friends. This works far better if you introduce them when they are at the kitten and puppy stage and is a great option for those people looking for a companion for their lone puppy—they can choose a kitten.

During my days as manager of an animal shelter, we would often place an orphaned puppy with an orphaned kitten. The bonus of this matching was that the kitten would very quickly housetrain the puppy, teaching it to use the litter tray.

So if you 're bringing a puppy/dog home to a household that already has a cat, then you will need to introduce them correctly, with puppy/dog on lead, with no fuss and with great care, making sure to correct any aggression or barking from the dog. Don't rush the process—if the cat runs or moves away, don't stress, just try again the next day and so on till they both relax. Off-lead fraternisation will take time, so be patient. You will know when they're ready to coexist without fights.

Other pets and stock animals

Other pets and stock animals are generally easier as they are usually confined or can be confined, making the introduction process easier. In general use the same process as detailed in the cat introduction, go about feeding your other pets, keeping your puppy or dog near you and on lead as you go, correcting any unwanted behaviour, until they become more accepting. Never allow your puppy or dog off the lead until you are very sure that he won't rush off and chase or attack the pet. This would quickly undo all of your good work.

Bark Busters say:

- When introducing dogs and cats, always control the dog, allowing the cat free range, and a peace can be brokered quite quickly.

- Always place the dog on-lead, correcting any unwanted behaviour.

- When introducing your puppy or dog to any animal on your property, place your puppy or dog on-lead, taking them with you when you feed your other pets, correcting any unwanted behaviour.

- Do not allow your puppy or dog off-lead near your other pets till you are sure that they won't chase them.

18 Have Dog, Will Travel

🐾 Sox's paws for thought

Dogs – travel broadens the nasal passages
Humans – travel broadens the mind

Or will you? Some of us love a spin in the Holden; others run a mile at the first jangle of the car keys. Interestingly, Snowy and I represent these two opposing opinions. As a senior member of the Car Crazy Canine Club (CCCC), you can tell which side of the driveway I sit.

In contrast, the idea of being cooped up in a metal 'death box' can bring on a meltdown in Snowy. You couldn't get two more disparate views, which is perfect if you wanted to write a chapter about cars and canines!

Automobile amour

Oh, cars, how do I love thee? Let me count the ways. I love thee to the depth and breadth and height of your tyres. To a dog, a tyre is a highly concentrated, chaotic scent ball, offering a tantalising nasal insight of the exotic world outside the fence. There is an art to successful tyre sniffing. It takes time to unravel the mysteries of the odours from afar, but for the dedicated the rewards are there; a squashed honey bee, the tang of the sea and loads of unknown doggy wee. Car-obsessed humans, please note: the ubiquitous leg lift is simply a reciprocal baptismal pee, not a deliberate attempt to rust your beloved rims.

Moving ever upwards, we come to the all important vehicle body. While utes offer an open air ride, with great vision and the benefits of unlimited sniffing, there is always the chance of rain. Hard core ute dogs are a pretty tough lot, so the idea of wet whiskers doesn't appear to faze them. Snowy has a theory about these dogs which suggests the size of the tray is inversely proportional to the size of their tails. As I've done my share of ute riding, I'm not going to comment, other than to say I prefer the covered ride these days. My favourite is the 4WD cab. It gives me my own space, but still allows for human interaction. Simply resting there instills me with a feeling of contentment—my very own Zen garden. Don't even mind where we drive. It is all about the journey, not the destination.

At a recent CCCC meeting, I asked the members exactly why they were car fanciers. Here are some of the more memorable quotes:

> *What's not to like? They play hard and go fast. (Rex the Rottweiler)*

> *I love them, whatever love means. (Charlie, the King Charles Spaniel)*

> *Car travel is the only way to go. Walking is so common. (Camilla Barker Bowls, the Chihuahua)*

> *My human and I like to cruise the streets in the ute. It's 100% mean machine. (Arni, the Pekingese)*

To be honest, my love affair with the Cruiser has caused issues. If there's a possible trip in the air, my brain turns to mush and this intelligent dog becomes a whining, whimpering whinger. Drives (paw pun alert) my humans mad and even Snowy complains about my 'obsession' (and this from a Terrier). Once I'm in, I don't like to budge, for anyone or anything (yes, Snowy, I was just getting to that)…even if it means being dressed up as a 'baby', with rattle and lacey bonnet by those young girls. (See, there was no public humiliation. Just proves I am comfortable in my own fur and dog enough to indulge in a little human dressing without embarrassment.)

Automobile anxiety

Snowy's fear of cars and travelling has proved to be much more dysfunctional and debilitating than my simple car crazies. As with many behaviour issues, it all started way back in the dim dark days of her puppyhood. Her very first car trip was marked (figuratively and literally) by her very first vomit:

> *I had been looking forward to obedience class for weeks. The night finally arrived and as I leapt into the car seat, I was full of excitement, trepidation...and chunky beef casserole. In the short trip to the park, I lost none of my excitement, but most of my dinner. Luckily my aim was true and the offending vomit was neatly wrapped in the towel and thrown in the boot. Alas, the whole sorry affair repeated itself on the return journey but this time there was no protective towel. Even I was surprised by the sheer volume of food my small tummy regurgitated. Of course, it wasn't my fault and if they had taken a sample like I suggested...*

Sorry, had to put my paw down and stop her. Even after years of suffering motion sickness, Snowy can't accept responsibility for her actions. She maintains the food is off or poisoned or otherwise tampered with every time the car vomit is brought up...I mean mentioned. If there was half a brain rattling around in that vacant head of hers, she would understand the reason behind the 'heaving hound' is a malfunctioning of the inner ear, not a plot by the Rodent League to discredit her. Pity my kennel mate is so vehemently against travel. She could well do with a bit of mind broadening.

At one stage my humans got a crazy idea about putting Snowy into a carry basket inside the car, rather than letting her stay free and wild. The basket was supposed to represent a safe, dark retreat, but was not a success. One sniff told us it had been used for feline cartage in a previous life. Snowy was unimpressed, as any decent dog would be. Then there was the issue of her claustrophobia. You would think that Fox Terrier and claustrophobia were mutually exclusive, but this was not the case. She maintains that the very thought of going to ground can bring on a panic attack. Good news for our local rodents, but not for Snowy's credibility. I believe if this was inadvertently made public—in a book for example—she risks being struck off the Terrier register.

After this, trips for Snowy were whittled down to the yearly vet visits. I'm sure my humans meant to be kind, but honestly! They have created a classic fear conditioning situation which reinforces all the negative associations Snowy already has about cars. To her small brain, the jangle of keys means thrusting thermometers, needles and bitter tablets. No wonder it also produces a dribbling, panting, whining wreck of a dog.

Travelling with your furry friend

So, for dogs like me, a driving holiday is a joy. The wanderlust for the open road isn't a purely human emotion. We put in long hard hours of toil on our humans behalf and deserve a break as much as you. Just remember to check the holiday destination is dog friendly and has the paw of approval before you head off into the wild blue yonder. Follow my tips for stress free and fun filled travel with your pooch:

Sox's Simple Solutions

- Dogs are precious – secure us safely with a harness or seat belt.
- Don't forget our food bowls and leads.
- Never leave us inside a parked car, it gets way too hot.
- Give us plenty of park stops to stretch our four legs and indulge in copious weeing and random scent marking (drives the local mutts mad).

• Dogs love rushing air and the cornucopia of road smells (motorbike riders will understand), so leave the window down a little.

Not travelling with your furry friend

So what happens when holiday time arrives and you have a boring, stop-in dog like Snowy? Leaving them home alone, with a can opener and a week's supply of tinned food just isn't going to work (lack of opposable thumb, remember!). Getting a reliable, responsible 'dog friendly' human to live in at the house is a great idea. Maybe they won't know the sofa is out of bounds...hmmm this has definite possibilities which Snowy can pursue. Staying with dogcentric friends or relatives is also an option. My human's kindhearted father always makes us feel welcome on his property. The whole experience is five-paw luxury. Bush walks, wild animal smells, fresh manure to roll in, our very own (human) beds to snuggle into, warm porridge for breakfast—the best home away from home a dog could want.

My least favourite option is a boarding kennel or 'dog motel' as they are euphemistically called (so where are those natty little soaps and biscuit packs I ask?). Check these places out carefully before you blithely drop us off. Look for clean, warm and pleasant smelling. That's the proprietors taken care of, but the same applies to the kennels. The problem with these places is they aren't home and many bear an uncanny resemblance to 'the pound'. Take a favourite toy and blankey to ease your dog's loneliness. Snowy and I have so far avoided 'boarding', but a number of friends have not been so lucky. Benji goes in annually and urges caution:

> Choose the kennel carefully. There's a huge range of quality, from the sublime to the shoddy. One year I got caught up in an illicit toad licking group. Bufo marinus parties proliferated and the practice spread through the kennel like a flea plague in summer. Too many anxious

dogs locked up together searching for answers—there's bound to be problems. Lucky I was picked up before things escalated.

Travelling shouldn't be stressful or unpleasant. If you have an anti-travel 'Snowy' type dog, forget all those notions of romping on the beach with your canine companion as the sun sinks beneath the waves. Leave them behind. Everyone (humans and dogs) will be happier. However, if you are lucky enough to have an itchy-pawed 'Sox' type, do everything you can to include them in family outings and trips. They deserve it!

All work and no travel makes Sox a dull dog.

The Human Perspective on Car Travel

As a professional trainer and also as the owner of two dogs with completely opposite views of the car ride, I know exactly what Sox is talking about. Kayla would jump into the car with relish, whereas my other dog Diesel would look as though he was about to face a firing squad.

Some dogs love cars and go into excited yelping, barking and leaping about at the prospect of a ride (another problem we get called upon to fix), whereas others run for their kennel, hide under the bed or shake from head to foot each time they hear the car keys jingle. These dogs will either begin to salivate as soon as they enter the car (remembering past trips) or throw up due to motion sickness.

It can be upsetting for those humans who love driving if they have a dog that refuses to accompany them on a road trip, or if their dog becomes sick when they go out. We receive many calls for help for this problem, and fortunately we have many solutions. There are several ways to solve your dog's 'car aversion'. First you have to understand the reasons that your dog might want to avoid getting into your car. Some dogs, as described by Sox, suffer from inner ear problems that may cause them to become sick. Your vet might prescribe travel sickness tablets, if the middle ear is the underlying problem.

Another thing that can cause car sickness is the amount of static electricity that your car produces. Some dogs are very sensitive to static electricity but there are fairly easy ways to resolve this. You could try a 'doggy coat' that has been lined with an anti-static material. I have found that brown paper works quite well. I don't really know why this works, but suspect that it stops the static electricity affecting the dog's tummy. I also recommend that people acquire an anti-static car mat that your dog can lie on, as well as an anti-static strip that hangs off the back of the car that acts to earth the car. Both products are available from car accessory shops.

Another reason why some dogs hate cars is that their first car experience was traumatic, and they remember it every time they see the car. Maybe they went to the vet for an injection, or visited a doggy park or stayed at a boarding kennel and hated the experience. Dogs learn by repetition and association, so once they've had a bad experience, they always think the same thing will happen each time they enter that car. Because of the way dogs are wired, they think that this experience will occur again and again, so you have to work at wiping the 'unpleasant thought' out of their mind and attempt to create a pleasant association in its place, all centred around the car.

I have had some great success with dogs that hated travelling in cars by using a number of techniques. One was to have owners feed their dog in the car. This would work towards changing the dynamics in the dog's mind, eventually removing the negative association with the car. Another technique I recommend is that the owners take their dog on a long trip (for over an hour), allowing them to settle in, then making sure that they went to their dog's favourite place (such as the beach or Grandma's house) at the end of the journey.

Auto Immune Rueben

Rueben, a Great Dane that was rescued from an animal welfare shelter, was a serious case of 'car aversion'. He was taken to the shelter as a very young puppy and was the last of the litter to find a home. He was fully grown when he was finally adopted, and it took five people to get him into the car so his new owners could take him home.

From that day on, it became impossible for his owners to get him back in the car, even with the help of several people. When we were called in, we worked at showing the owner through consistency and basic training, to become Rueben's alpha human. We also suggested that eventually Rueben should be fed only in the car and nowhere else, advising that they started out by feeding him in the garage near the car, building on this till they could place the food inside the car.

This was designed to change Rueben's association with the car from unpleasant to pleasant, and something not to be feared. Eventually with patience and time, Reuben's owners were able to get him into the car and then take him for a ride. We recommended only short trips at first, with no stopping along the way, and returning straight home. Then gradually they would take longer trips to places he loved, followed by much longer trips. He now travels happily with his humans, his previous bad experiences now a distant memory.

Bark Busters say:

- If you have a dog that becomes sick when travelling in your car, your vet may prescribe travel sickness tablets.

- If static electricity is the problem, try an anti-static mat, car earthing strip or a doggy coat lined with anti-static material.

- If your dog has unpleasant memories of its first car trip, then alter the dynamics in the dog's mind by creating a pleasant experience based around the car, such as feeding your dog in the car or taking your dog for a long trip to a place they love.

19 The Golden Years

The whole world loves a puppy, which means the focus of many canine books is on the youngsters. I intend to dog paddle against this tide of opinion and declare my support for the golden oldies. This is something I touched on in Chapter One. It seems fitting that I continue with my doggy dotage discourse on this, the very last chapter of the book.

I am a mature canine of 12 and Snowy turns 16 next birthday. If we don't know a thing or two about the trials and treasures of being older dogs, I don't know who does. The other reason for devoting a whole chapter on the golden years is that dogs of a certain age are so interesting, with our quirks and foibles. Just ask my co-author (a human with excellent taste):

> *Puppies are very cute, but I much prefer the older dog, one that has developed a personality, full of eccentricity and idiosyncrasies.*

It is not my intention to make broad sweeping generalisations about the older dog (bury that thought!), other than to state we are 100% superior to our younger compatriots. So, exactly why is it so? Having left the hurly burly of puppyhood and the influence of 'pack pressure' long behind us, we are the perfect low-maintenance canine companion.

Older dogs:

- don't chew things up (lack of teeth)
- do prefer hot dinners to hot bitches/dogs (lack of ardour)
- don't chase the postie (lack of inclination)
- do prefer a park perambulation to the morning marathon (lack of energy)

You'll also be pleased to hear that toileting tribulations are a thing in the past with the mature dog. We are fully trained in pee protocol. No more inside accidents, wet carpets, puddles in the lounge…(alright Snow, it will get mentioned, but I want it made absolutely clear I have complete control over my bladder and it was the hose, ok?) unless your dog suffers from an embarrassing incontinence problem.

Of course, the life of the ageing dog isn't just a walk in the park and even the facetious philosopher has to admit there are some drawbacks to getting old. At the risk of being labelled a boring old whiner, here is a quick rundown on my experiences as a senior canine.

My clean and virtuous life has rewarded me with excellent health. Apart from yearly vaccinations (and the previously mentioned 4WD incident) I avoided any extra vet visits. Snowy was a different kettle of Terrier. If I told her once, I told her a thousand times, that reckless lifestyle would catch up on her— and it did. What with the tick paralysis and snake bites (too much bush snuffling), damaged cruciate ligaments and torn claws (too much vigorous soccer), skin cancers and growths (too much sun worshipping) she was a clinic regular, just as *moi* predicted. (I refute the accusation of smarmy, sanctimonious goody four paws. It's just that I care.)

Unfortunately, once I turned 10, things started to go pear shaped (or ball shaped to be exact). Distinctive round body 'sculptures' began to develop on my chest. Naturally, I assumed these were bulging muscles. When the lumps began to appear in more unusual spots, like my tummy, I started to worry. These turned out to be fatty deposits, a type of benign tumour, common in older, overweight dogs—much to Snowy's delight. The official term is lipomas, which I prefer. These lipomas were the start of a slippery slope downhill. Next up was my spleen, which was whipped out before I could bark Jack Russell. On the plus side, I weighed that bit less, which to a biggish dog, has to be a good thing. Just as I was settling down to a life post spleen, I was hit with a dose of pancreatitis. I was sick as the proverbial dog. Damn you bacon rind! The week at the vet convinced me to dig over a new leaf. Fatty foods were off the menu.

As we matured, my kennel mate and I adopted the 'work smarter, not harder' adage to counteract our reduced energy levels (Sox-speak for getting old and indolent). The potential burglar run to the bottom of the yard is all very well. Coming back up, not so great. Guarding duties, including regular checks of the perimeter fence are shared, thus allowing the 'off duty' dog to indulge in some well earned R and R (or creative writing pursuits). At the first sign of trouble, a quick woof brings back up and the enemy is confronted by a united front of canines. At times, we will admit to 'not seeing' the human, dog or magpie go past. This is when the mind is willing, but the flesh weak. Naturally, this oversight never applies to the feline species and if any cat thinks the four-legged philosopher and his assistant have gone weak, just let them try to cross our territory—then we'll see who's elderly and infirm!

As we're on the subject of energy levels, I must mention our afternoon walks which have been correspondingly curtailed. Previously, we would do the three-kilometre trek ending in a hill climb. This was fine for strapping young dogs, full of vim and vigour. For an elderly canine of generous figure, it all got too much (yes, Snowy, you are elderly, but no, you don't have a generous figure and yes, I'm sure you've still got what it takes). Thankfully, my humans have moved us on to a more manageable one-kilometre ramble. There are still plenty of trees, poles and grass stalks to pee-read and christen with our own news, but it is a pleasanter way to while away the afternoon.

The good news on ageing dogs is we don't sprout unattractive hairy bits from our ears, like some human males I've seen. Well, extra hairy bits, that is. The bad news is dogs do go deaf. In the ultimate point score for yours truly, deafness is more common in white dogs, than black. (Sox 1, Snowy 0). The combination of deaf and ditzy in a dog results in some very unusual behaviour:

I admit to not hearing the telltale tinkle of cat bells like I used to. To overcome this, I spend my free time in Barker's Corner, yapping madly in the direction of the neighbour's yard, in case of lurking cats. Sox may refer to it as 'brainless woofing, by a brainless dog'. I like to call it a pre-emptive strike at the feline heartland. After a solid half hour barkfest, I need a drink of water and a good lie down to recover. Then it's back into Barker's Corner for more of the same.

(Snowy 'The Bones' Osborne)

Snowy may be hearing – and brain – impaired, but, unlike me, she has avoided the old-age affliction of arthritis. She is as jaunty as ever and her step has lost none of its sparkle, whereas I hobble around in the cold weather, giving rise to the nickname 'Sore Paw Sox'. Snowy likes to push the 'overweight dog is an arthritic dog' theory, but I prefer to believe it was the luck of genetics. As well as painful joints, my arthritis made jumping into the back of my beloved Landcruiser a herculean effort. Even taking a running leap didn't help. After a number of embarrassing miscalculations, my humans built a natty little ramp to assist me. Not that Snowy uses it. She stands at the bottom with that pathetic, slow Terrier tail wag that my human can't resist. Her version is she 'doesn't do' dog ramps. My belief is that she 'doesn't understand' dog ramps. Which brings me to my next point—Snowy's brain drain.

I'm the first to admit Snowy has aged well—on the outside. Apart from the odd silver streak marring her black spots and a couple of beauty warts sprouting proudly from her chin, life has been kind to her. Cousin Chloe is the same vintage, but the gummy smile, rheumy eyes and patchy coat make her look positively raddled in comparison. So, if age has not wearied her physically, what about mentally? Peer into Snowy's rather vacant head and suddenly the answer's clear, because all those brain atrophying free radicals have been very busy on her grey matter. Very busy indeed. And frankly, if you're not starting from a position of strength, losing even a few brain cells can't be good. Snowy's never been the sharpest bone in the backyard, so it's lucky she has me—the intellectual giant of the canine world—to help her through the puzzles of life. (Say, which way does the dog door swing again, Sox?)

So when does a dog know they have reached that time of life when they are 'senior'? For me, the realisation hit last week. A window of opportunity presented itself (the gate to the outside world was wide open). Here was a chance to run with the midnight pack, to feel the rush of the wind on my muzzle, to chase cats unfettered by the shackles of servitude and to howl at the moon as my ancestors did. Yes, the call of the wild was strong that night, but the call of din dins and my own sweet bed was stronger. I nudged the gate closed and headed inside.

Great dogs from little puppies grow.

The Human Perspective on the Older Dog

Compared to humans and other animals, dogs walk on this earth for a relatively short time. To my way of thinking, this makes them incredibly precious. You can get a clearer picture of the difference between dogs and humans if you work on the fact that one year of a dog's life is equivalent to approximately seven years of a human's. Although some dogs like Snowy live to a ripe old age, many don't. The bluebloods of the species are doing well if they reach 13 or 14 years of age, but the standard is 11 to 12 years for a purebred dog.

I have had 10 purebred dogs that have shared my life over a 40-year span that have reached ages ranging from 11 to 14 years of age. There are cases of bitsers/crossbreds reaching well over 20 years of age, so without a doubt, dogs of indiscriminate breeding, such as those found in abundance in animal welfare shelters, have the stronger genes for longevity and will generally enjoy a longer life.

The golden years are special years and ones we must treasure. Having a mature dog that behaves predictably, has learned that nuisance barking is unwarranted, knows where to toilet, has left the landscaping to the humans and finally realises that the neighbours are allowed to drive up their driveway unchallenged, is heady stuff and something all dog-loving humans aspire to achieve.

As our dogs age there are some things that we need to think about. One area is their diet, remembering, that like older humans, the ageing dog's digestive system will not be as effective as it was when they were younger. They may not be able to chew bones the way they used to, they might need softer, more easily digested food and might not need as much food due to their decreased levels of activity.

In providing a new diet to please your older dog I always recommend three small feeds of raw lamb or chicken mince (butcher shop or supermarket grade) half a teaspoon of fish oil, kelp, calcium and small amounts of blended raw veggies. There is also a high-quality packaged food available from vets and pet shops specifically designed for the older dog

Even though they might be less active, they still need mental stimulation. They may no longer want to chase balls, chew their rope toys or even get excited when you bring them their meal. However, as you'll see in the following case history of Sheba, you might need to reassess your dog's lifestyle as they reach their golden years.

Sheba the Sad Senior

My friend Jean consulted me about her 12 year old Rottweiler Sheba that was recovering from a recent operation to her left front leg. Jean's concern was that her dog now appeared to have lost the will to live.

On visiting Sheba I was saddened to see a very depressed dog. One problem was that she was spending a lot of time lying in her bed, only getting out to toilet. On checking her diet I discovered she was being fed on a low-quality dry food which she was largely rejecting, only choosing to eat one or two pieces a day. Her coat appeared dry, her eyes looked dull, devoid of any emotion, and her spirit was very low. This was a sad sight, and I told my friend that I was moving in for a few days to help her get Sheba well again.

We started her on small amount of apple cider vinegar in her drinking water to detox her system before changing her diet to something more appetising. To overcome Sheba's depression I recommended short walks outside of her yard, where she could sniff new smells and see a whole new outlook. The walks were designed to lift her spirits and prevent muscle wastage. Sheba was able to hop on three legs quite well and willingly went for short walks twice a day.

We also placed her on a diet of very small portions of minced lamb, fish oil, kelp, calcium and blended raw veggies three times a day. She began to eat again, her coat took on a shine, her eyes regained some of their sparkle and she was starting to wag her tail each time Jean came out to take her for her walks. Sheba quickly recovered and lived a happy healthy life for another two and a half years.

Bark Busters say:

• As your dog approaches the golden years, you might think about changing their diet to one that is easy to digest and one that excites their tastebuds.

• If your 'golden years' dog becomes depressed after surgery or illness, then give thought to his mental state and work at lifting his spirits through gentle exercise.

• Just because your ageing dog is less active doesn't mean he can't find interest in short walks or new places; an exercise regime suited to their capabilities is very important to their overall well being.

THE FINAL BARK

What a rollicking roller coaster of a ride *Dog Logic* has proved to be, both for my human assistant and me, the Philosophical Pooch. That it was created at all is tangible evidence of what can be achieved when the human and canine species collaborate (I still curse my lack of opposable thumbs). It is also testament to our efforts—we worked like dogs. My months of 'channelling' ideas to my human were both intellectually challenging and exhilarating. Of course, it was not all plain sailing. There were days of writer's block and self doubt, but the restorative powers of a good chicken feed and tummy rub got me through these dark times. When the last of *Dog Logic* wove its way to my assistant upstairs and on to the computer, I was a dog replete. My lifelong ambition had been realised. I had created a book which gave the reader a better insight into canine life, in all its intricacies and manifestations. A book which, ultimately, we hope will strengthen the bond between humans and canines just that little bit more. My human and I had a celebratory whine together and toasted the future.

BARK BUSTERS

Want a well behaved dog? Bark Busters say you can have one.

An Australian company founded by Sylvia and Danny Wilson, Bark Busters assists desperate owners with unruly pets in an effort to save dogs from being surrendered or euthanised. Sadly, something that during Sylvia's 10 years managing a RSPCA shelter she had seen far too much of, dogs in their prime, surrendered due to behaviour problems that could, with assistance be resolved. In 1989 they sold their home and started Bark Busters Home Dog Training.

Over the past 21 years Bark Busters has assisted over 500,000 dogs and their owners – their motto being 'any dog, any age and any problem'. Bark Busters is now the largest and most trusted dog training company in the world with over 500 offices spread across 10 countries around the globe.

Knowing how to educate a dog is not a skill that comes naturally to all dog owners. This can result in many behaviour problems-barking, digging, pulling, jumping up, not returning when called, aggression, toileting, separation anxiety, sibling rivalry and more. So whether you are the proud owner of a puppy, a dog who could do with a little help or a rebellious pooch, Bark Busters is your ticket to sanity.

Like people, dogs have their own personalities and idiosyncrasies and no two dogs are the same. Bark Busters assess each dog and tailor a programme to suit their personality. They show you how to communicate with your dog in a language that it can understand. Using a dog friendly approach, they work at gaining harmony in the household.

The techniques used by Bark Busters are astoundingly simple, effective and time-efficient and are also designed to work in tandem with a dog's natural instincts, without using bribery or any harsh methods. Most dogs' behaviour improves in one or two lessons.

Bark Busters come to your home at a suitable time and conduct 'In Home Dog Training' with you and your beloved pooch. Our 'Life of the Dog' guarantee is far superior to other dog training companies and offers owners peace of mind. Should further help be needed after the final consultation, clients ring Bark Busters who will return the call free of charge to provide further assistance. This guarantee is also transferable anywhere in the world, wherever there is a Bark Busters office.

The organisation has earned a well-respected reputation for its ability to get results where others fail. Bark Busters' aim is to make dog ownership the pleasurable experience it should be. Since 2008 SPCA International (USA) has named Bark Busters, the 'Best of the Best for Excellence in Behaviour Training' for three years in a row.

For more info on Bark Busters training or to discuss your dog's problem contact Bark Busters Australia on free call 1800 067710. www.barkbusters.com.au

Other Titles from Big Sky Publishing

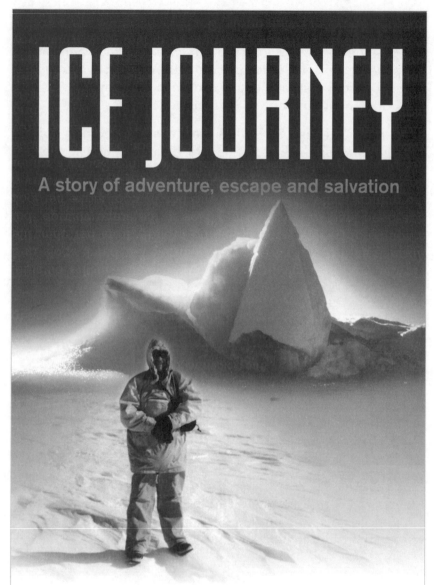

ICE JOURNEY

A story of adventure, escape and salvation

Dave Morgan

Available at all good bookstores or online
at www.bigskypublishing.com.au

"I was a 52-year-old man, married with two teenage children, trying to get down to Antarctica. "Everyone has an Antarctica", Thomas Pynchon once wrote. As a young bloke standing on the edge of a windy, wintery Melbourne beach...I just knew, staring towards the cold vastness of the Southern Ocean, that one day I'd go beyond the horizon."

Ice Journey is the biography of Vietnam veteran and Antarctica expeditioner Dave Morgan, a self confessed ordinary bloke who has led anything but an ordinary life.

Like many of his fellow Vietnam vets, Dave tried to present a "normal" face to the world while battling Post Traumatic Stress Disorder (PTSD). It was a debilitating struggle that sparked an obsession to escape the bonds of suburban Australia and embark on a journey to Antarctica; an experience that would change his life forever.

In his early fifties, Dave turned to the seclusion and hardship of Antarctic research, securing highly sought postings to Macquarie Island then Davis and Casey Stations. Carrying his deeply buried demons from the jungles of Vietnam to the icy peaks of Antarctica, Dave's journey fulfilled a lifelong dream, the peace of the ice making him feel safe for the first time in 30 years.

His experiences as an expeditioner on the starkly beautiful, harsh and inhospitable "Ice" were at once intoxicating and isolating, providing the catalyst for Dave to finally face his fears. It is an emotional journey that transports the reader from the terror of a young soldier fighting far away from home to exhilaration and adventure far from the rest of the world.

While the ghosts of Vietnam still exist for Dave, Ice Journey is an invitation to share his experiences, including the final heart-breaking twist that ultimately helped him stop running and finally begin to heal.

RRP: $29.99, Paper Back, 304 pages

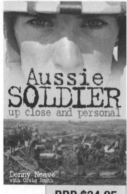

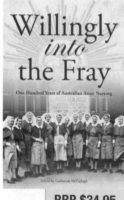
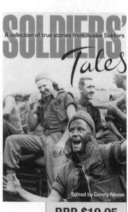
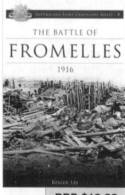

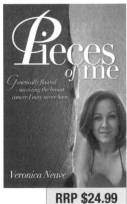

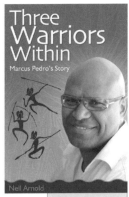